The National Theatre

The Touch of Silk

(1928)

Betty Roland

The Touch of Silk

(1928)

Betty Roland

Edited by Jonathan Shaw
Preface by A.D. Hope

Currency Press • Sydney

First published in 1942 by Melbourne University Press
in association with Oxford University Press, Melbourne
Revised edition published in 1974 by Currency Methuen Drama Pty Ltd
This revised edition first published in 1986 by Currency Press,
PO Box 2287, Strawberry Hills, NSW, 2012, Australia
enquiries@currency.com.au; www.currency.com.au

Reprinted 2000, 2001, 2004, 2014, 2022

NATIONAL LIBRARY OF AUSTRALIA CIP DATA

    Roland, Betty, 1903–1996
    The touch of silk
    I. Title   A822.3

Publication of this title was assisted by the Commonwealth
Government through the Australia Council, its arts funding and
advisory body.

General Editor's Preface

As the series title will suggest, the National Theatre is designed to represent the continuing vitality of Australian writing for the theatre since colonial times. The lack of readily available texts has in the past obscured not only the qualities but even the existence of our older drama, so that in turn we have been deprived of an historical context in which to assess contemporary play writing. Lacking such a context, we have perhaps concentrated critical attention too simply on comparative standards as opposed to comparative qualities; we have been more concerned to establish the stature of the Australian work vis a vis European models than to elicit the distinctive qualities through which the mirror is held up to the nature we know and, uniquely, need to understand. There is a sense in which the work that emanates from an immediate and familiar world is more important than the masterpiece expressing a different culture. And there is a sense in which the reverse is true. We need, of course, to be aware of both. In the past we have been more accessible to the latter.

The National Theatre, then, is not a classic series in the usual sense. It will, of course, include works of outstanding quality, but that will not be the sole criterion invoked. Rather, the series will consist of plays which, in the judgment of their editors, claim a place in a national Australian repertory—plays which demand revival in today's theatre because they express memorably something of the Australian experience in an eminently playable form. Though the very fact of publication will seem to throw the emphasis on dramatic literature, these texts are offered primarily as plays.

Most of the texts appearing in this series will not previously have been edited, many not even published, and very few of their authors have attracted extensive critical or biographical attention. Full–dress scholarly publication would in most cases involve a quite impractical labour of research; nor, perhaps, is the time yet quite ready, given the fairly limited present extent of Australian dramatic scholarship. What will be attempted here, there–fore, is a reliable foundation for future work. A text will be established and the editorial grounds made clear, drafts and revisions will be collated and major variants annotated. The series is, however, intended to render important plays available to a more general readership than the specialist scholar, so the text will be kept clear of marginal line numbers, footnotes, and other apparatus which may smack of the schoolroom. It is hoped that the interested scholar will accept the burden of counting lines in consulting the text from the notes gathered at the back of the book.

Since texts will range over more than a century of Australian drama, involving very different editorial problems, each editor will be left with wide freedom to arrive at an appropriate disposition of supporting material about the text. He may, for instance, invite outside contribution for the introduction or for specialist factual appendices. The one guiding principle will be to make the play as accessible as possible in the imaginative sense. Whatever the format adopted to meet individual circumstances, the edition will include a discussion of the play and of its place within the work of its author, together with some biographical account of the author. Where appropriate, comment will be made on the stage history and staging of the play. When textual notes are necessary, they will be gathered separately from explanatory notes, which are chiefly concerned with contemporary references.

PHILIP PARSONS
Sydney, 1973

Contents

Currency Press acknowledges the Traditional Owners of the Country on which we live and work. We pay our respects to all Aboriginal and Torres Strait Islander Elders, past and present.

Preface

In deciding to reprint *The Touch of Silk* the publishers have been faced with a dilemma. It is an old play now, a famous old play even though it first appeared in 1928, not long as dramatic history goes. But the intervening years have seen such extra–ordinary changes in the theatre, and in the Australian theatre above all, that in some respects the play has become outdated—though it has lost little of its original vitality and of the stage effect which have led to its being revived a good many times in past years. Feeling this, Betty Roland has recently re–written the play and produced a more easily moving, up–to–date and from an acting point of view a more streamlined version, if I may so express it. It was of course natural that the author should wish to see the improved and later version of the play in print. But I am pleased that she has agreed to the preference of the publishers for reprinting the original. I am pleased, too, that enough sections of the new version have been included in the annotations to allow readers to form an impression of it and of the sorts of change the author has made to her earlier work.

I am pleased in the first place because, as I say, *The Touch of Silk* is quite a famous play now and something of a landmark in the history of Australian drama. It is described and commented on in histories of Australian drama, Australian theatre and Australian literature both as an outstanding play of its period and as significant of the progress of dramatists in this country at the time and of the problems they then had to face. To have printed a new version would have been misleading to students and critics of Australian drama who are not lucky enough to possess copies of the original edition, which has long been out of print. And, in addition, the play would have lost a good deal of its period flavour, which I for one cherish with the nostalgia of my generation for their own yesterdays. But it will be increasingly interesting for new generations to catch this flavour which is perhaps best of all preserved in art and literature. It is they who put flesh on the bones of history.

Between the early years of this century and the nineteen fifties Australian dramatists were faced with a serious problem. Before this time a small but vigorous Australian drama had been growing up and there were theatres and a theatre–going public to support it. Within a decade all this had vanished. The cinema proved such a rival to the stage that theatre after theatre closed down in the 'twenties and 'thirties, while those that remained constituted a monopoly. They only staged plays which had been a marked success in London or New York, and often imported the cast as well as the play. The result was that the Australian dramatist was largely cut off from an audience except in the few repertory theatres that then existed. These never, as they did in America, flourished to the extent that they could promote and establish an Australian drama. At most they enabled dramatists to keep a precarious toe–hold in the theatre and they never, of course, made enough money to enable a writer to become a dramatist by profession. The great economic depression of the 'thirties added to that already operating in the drama itself and things reached their lowest ebb just before the Second World War. The war improved things to the extent that it cut off the supply of imported plays and imported theatre companies from abroad, and between 1940 and 1950 things began to improve until the foundation of the Australian Elizabethan Theatre Trust in 1954 began a new era in all the arts of the theatre.

The Touch of Silk in some measure illustrates the disabilities under which dramatists were working in the 'thirties and 'forties. Good plays are not as a rule produced in a vacuum or even in the author's study. They require a working knowledge of the theatre. The dramatist learns his craft in the course of rehearsal and production. He learns how to write for a live audience by studying that audience's reaction to his plays on the stage. And he learns how to write dialogue that has the economy, the immediacy and the ease that good drama demands by association with professional actors and producers, whose manipulation of his text and changes in his script and in the details of his imagined action are the dramatist's real schooling. Of course he can learn something from a repertory production of his play, but the limitation is that Australain repertory companies are rarely professional and they rarely help the novice to get beyond his amateur status. The result is obvious in the plays written by most Australian dramatists up to the nineteen fifties. Whatever their virtues, they are all in a sense rather amateurish in their handling of plot and dialogue, and in realising the stage possibilities and the theatrical pitfalls of their scenes and themes.

A clear example of this is the handling of the machinery on which the dramatic situation and development of *The Touch of Silk* depends. In the old version the young farmer, Jim, has borrowed money to buy extra property and to stock it, against the security of his own and his mother's farm. His reason for this is largely to give his young French wife a better sort of life than the one he has grown up to. A drought, however, forces him to sell some of his stock and Alexander Ritchie, the shopkeeper in the little country town from whom he borrowed the money, is threatening to foreclose if Jim cannot keep up the payments. But if he does he cannot afford to send the remainder of his stock to his uncle in Gippsland. So either way he will be ruined. As dramatic machinery this is a creaky device straight out of Victorian melodrama and Ritchie is a stock melodrama villain. One cannot help wondering why Jim has not gone to the bank in the first instance—and now, when Ritchie threatens to fore–close, why, as the owner of two properties, he doesn't go and see his bank manager. The sum involved is only fifty pounds. And of course there is the uncle in Gippsland with enough property to take Jim's starving stock. One imagines he might be able to help to the extent of fifty pounds with the stock as security. The whole thing has the air of amateurish construction. In the new version all this has been competently revised. The original agreement with Ritchie is given in full on the stage. Ritchie is a more credible character. Jim naturally thinks of the bank but is led to believe that Ritchie is offering him a better deal and the uncle in Gippsland has been dropped. This more sophisticated and workmanlike construction is matched by dialogue which runs more naturally and more in the idiom of the talk and ideas of rural districts. The dialogue of the older version has a certain stiffness about it which, in the later version, the author's experience in the theatre and in writing plays for radio has enabled her to eliminate.

Nevertheless I do not want to give the impression that the old version is simply crude. It moves *swiftly*, it is convincing and it is more complex in its theme than it looks at first sight. The obvious theme is that of the French girl, fresh from Europe, the civilisation of a great capital, cut off from all the life she has known and confronted with a drought–stricken countryside and a hayseed community, tempted to a little luxury and bringing disaster on the only thing she has to live by, her love for her husband. On this plane it is a simple but moving tragedy. But on another plane it touches the lives of so many Australians of the 'twenties and 'thirties, for whom the war had meant a glimpse of a larger world and a higher culture. Jeanne, of course, is Jim's touch of silk and she is his extravagance as the silk underwear is hers.

Indeed, in a way, the play is strangely prophetic of the situation of so many of the Europeans who flocked to Australia before and during the Second World War and who in various ways enriched and changed our culture. *The Touch of Silk* is a play which, if performed today, has overtones that were only just beginning to be heard when the play was written. This is only one of the reasons that it has continued to hold audiences and to maintain its charm and its vitality.

A. D. HOPE
Canberra, 1974

Introduction

i

Betty Roland

The Touch of Silk was applauded for its very real virtues in 1928, and has rarely been mentioned without honour since. Its reputation, won in the 'little theatres' in various kinds of amateur productions, has been tested with professional actors only on radio. Its author too has been caught in the painful paradox of being by profession a playwright without a professional theatre to write for. Both play and playwright, like so many others of their time, found a public through the radio rather than on the stage.

Mary Isobel Maclean was born at Kaniva, a small town in the Mallee district of north–west Victoria, the only daughter of the local doctor, Roland Maclean. Her father died when she was four years old, and she was taken by her mother to live on her maternal grandfather's property near Nagambie in the Goulburn Valley. Although she was to be educated mainly in Melbourne and has spent most of her adult life in cities, the importance of these early environments to her imaginative life is evident from *The Touch of Silk* onwards[1]. Certainly, most of her fictional and dramatic works are set in the country.

Betty Maclean decided to become a writer while still at school. Encouraged in her resolution by a prize in a Ballarat short story competition, she entered the field of journalism, joining the *Melbourne Sun Pictorial* as a junior reporter in 1922. However, her marriage the following year to Ellis H. Davies, a consulting engineer, delayed the realisation of her literary ambitions for some years. A children's play called *The Gate of Bronze* and a dramatisation of *The Scarlet Pimpernel*, which were performed by pupils at The Hermitage Girls' Grammar School in Geelong in 1925, were the first indications of her talents as a playwright.

In 1928 she approached the newly appointed director of the Melbourne Repertory Theatre[2], Frank D. Clewlow[3], with the script of a play set in the Australian outback. Clewlow, a man of considerable experience in both professional and amateur theatre, made suggestions as to how the script might be expanded and modified, and later that same year he directed the first production of Betty M. Davies' *The Touch of Silk*. This play by a twenty–five year old housewife was an immediate success with the admittedly small public available to the Repertory Theatre, and was hailed as a landmark in the development of Australian drama[4]. But although it was taken up by other 'little theatres', the commercial managements showed no interest whatever.

The nett effect was to discourage her from further writing for the stage: in the next few years, her sole creative output was a one–act play set in the days of the first gold rushes, called *Morning*, which was produced in 1932 by Brett Randall at the Kiosk Theatre, Fawkner Park, Melbourne; and the beginnings of a three–act drama, *Granite Peak*. She was freshly stimulated when, after the termination of her marriage in 1933, she spent fifteen months in the Soviet Union working as a journalist and in publishing. Like so many others at that time, she was deeply impressed by the Russian venture, and it was in emulation of the Russian practice that she adopted her father's name and became Betty Roland. In Russia, too, she met Guido Baracchi, a prominent Australian Communist, with whom she formed a free relationship that endured until 1941.

Returning to Australia in 1935, she joined the Communist Party and devoted her dramatic talents to writing for agit–prop groups. Her short satirical plays on current political topics were performed on the Sydney Domain, on the Yarra Bank in Melbourne, and in numerous halls and factory yards. The only full–length play of her political period was *Are You Ready, Comrade?*, which won the 1938 West Australian Theatre Council competition for an original play. This drama about the politicisation of the young wife of an older ailing man was first performed at the Patch Theatre in Perth; Betty Roland played the heroine in the production at the New Theatre, Sydney, in 1939. This phase of her writing came to an end in the late 'thirties when first the Moscow trials—in which a number of her friends received savage sentences—and then the Stalin–Hitler pact disillusioned her regarding Communism. She left the Party and forswore politics, she says, forever.

The 'forties, the hey–day of Australian radio drama, she spent mainly in writing for radio, both the ABC and commercial stations. Since she now had a daughter to support, it is not surprising that she ran the whole gamut from full–length plays, soap operas and adaptations of plays and novels to talks on travel and 'women's topics'. Of her radio plays, the most noteworthy is *Daddy Was Asleep* (1945), in which the main dramatic interest lies in the relationship between the editor of a country newspaper and his daughter[5]. During this time, her only excursion into writing for the stage was an adaptation of Flaubert's *Madame Bovary* for the Independent Theatre, Sydney, where it was performed in 1946 with Doris Fitton in the title role.

In 1952, Betty Roland and her school–girl daughter went to London. While there, she re–wrote Granite Peak and sold it to Radio–Rediffusion as a television play. The production proved yet another discouraging experience: the largely non–Australian cast and British director failed to understand the Central Australian situation and characters, and the play was very poorly received. Discouraged, she decided to abandon the theatre and turn her attention to writing prose. By the time she returned to Australia in 1961, she was well established as a children's author, and went on to write several children's books and two travel books. Her first novel, *The Other Side of Sunset*, a straight–forward romance set in the outback, was published in 1972 by Mills & Boon, and a second, more substantial romance called *No Ordinary Man* by William Collins in 1974.

ii
The Touch of Silk: stage history

The Touch of Silk was first performed by the Melbourne Repertory Theatre at the Playhouse, Melbourne, on 3rd November 1928 with the following cast:

JEANNE	Lucy Ahon
MRS DAVIDSON	Betty Rae
MRS RYAN	Ruby May
MISS PATTERSON	Kathleen Salter
NELLY	Jack O'Keefe
JIM DAVIDSON	Hilary Blake
CLIFFORD OSBORNE	George Faulkner

DR WILSON	Claude Thomas
ALEXANDER RITCHIE	David Dorrity
CONSTABLE HUGHES	Philip Shaperc
DAVID RITCHIE	Russell Lamble
HARRY	Reg Moyle

The producer was Frank D. Clewlow[6].

It was a short season, five nights only, and the production was amateur, but press notices were without exception favourable[7]: the Melbourne *Herald*'s anonymous reviewer described it as "the first Australian play written by a real dramatist"; the Sydney *Bulletin* announced that "the birth of poor old Australian drama" had actually taken place at last. And it was not simply a matter of puffing the underprivileged local product. The *Herald* review, for example, went on to specify what it meant by "a real dramatist":

> We have had superior literary efforts. We have had two major and a few minor box office successess[8]. But here is the real grip—the real life of dramatic power and inspiration. It cannot have been a fluke... The plot is compounded of what, in other circumstances, we would immediately recognise and label as hackneyed stuff. The material could not make its own inspiration. And yet the whole thing is made to march with the rhythm, with the inevitableness that is the pattern of great drama... The real drama of the play is like the vein of gold that runs through the quartz lode...

Although rather unspecific—and the vein of gold is not more fully identified elsewhere in the review—this is not uncritical praise; and it has the virtue rare in Australian reviewers of attempting to relate the play to earlier dramatic writing, however fleetingly. The reviewer persuades us that his enthusiasm is not only genuine but informed. The *Herald*'s response was not exceptional, and the general acclaim led to the play having an unprecedented circulation among the little theatres. During the next two years, it was produced by the Brisbane and Adelaide Repertory Theatres and by the Turret Theatre in Sydney.

One need not look far for the reasons for this success. It is true that in literary terms the play leaves much to be desired: Professor Hope speaks of creakiness in the plot machinery and stiffness in the dialogue. It is also true that according to modern canons of taste, the play may seem quaint or naive: indeed in the 1970 version of the play Betty Roland has left hardly a single speech unaltered. But these are not necessarily faults in the theatre. Indeed, the play's record suggests otherwise: *The Touch of Silk*, a play of 1928, is full of strong situations that call for larger than life acting. It has the virtues of good melodrama.

Its one obvious strength is in the character of Jeanne, who from her first laughing appearance dominates the stage by sheer presence:

> *She gives one of her expressive gestures that seems to embrace the drab country store, the dull outlook of those with whom she is forced to associate, and holds them up in contrast with the great world from which she has come.*

The actress is required to make present as it were a whole lost world where mankind is at ease with the environment and society embraces the joyfulness of living. If the image of "the great world" as it emerges from the dialogue is somewhat inadequate, amounting to little more than burlesque theatres, restaurants and expensive lingerie, that is not necessarily a failing in the theatre, where the effect depends not solely on the words used—on the literary accomplishment—but on the total dramatic moment. Here, the situation is clearly enough structured, the rest is up to the actors. Moreover, the France of Jeanne and Clifford Osborne is important in the play precisely because it is absent. It becomes the type of all that is fine, graceful and generous, but beyond even the dreams of this drought–stricken land. Jeanne's nationality, her accent, is the sign of her allegiance to that absence; and her grace, her vitality, her generosity of spirit are the fruits of that allegiance.

It is Jeanne's play, perhaps, but not without a struggle. For Mrs. Davidson has her dramatic strengths as well. Although subjected to the indignity of funny hats and trivially vulgar preoccupations, she becomes more than a comic dragon lady and dominates the spiritual life of the town as surely as the elder Ritchie controls the financial. In a sense she is a child of the drought; in terms of Jeanne's crises, she is its most assiduous ally. "A dry arid shrimp of a woman", "shabby and toil–worn", she has denied herself much and bitterly rejects any expansiveness or indulgence in others. She is something of a bush philosopher: "It seems to me there's always something in this life to keep us from being happy," she says, and if the remark is occasioned by a boil on Mr. Ryan's backside, it is no less weighty for that. Her antagonism to Jeanne is not simply that of a jealous mother–in–law. The two women are engaged in a battle to possess the stage in the name of their respective world views, and in some ways Mrs. Davidson is the clear winner. Seen in the light of hard practical necessity, Jeanne's squandering of her money is astonishingly ungenerous, and her forgetting to tell Jim of the broken fence to the dam is unforgivable. Her very theatrical virtues are real vices: she is unable to relinquish the impossible and so jeopardises the actual. It is perhaps because of the justice of Mrs. Davidson's point of view that Jeanne's final desolation is so poignant: she has brought it on her own head. Her inability to make Mrs. Davidson's kind of daily renunciation leads to the necessity of her final renunciation of her one source of happiness, her husband's love.

All other interactions in the play are secondary to the conflict between Mrs. Davidson and Jeanne. Even Jim's anguished jealousy at the end of Act Two is subsidiary to Mrs. Davidson's realisation at that point of the effect of her words on him. Unusual anywhere, the central importance given to stresses between female characters surely makes this play extraordinary in the literature dealing with rural Australia, where so often relationships between men dominate to the exclusion of so much. The *Bulletin*, in a review of the Turret production in 1929, as laudatory as the original notice but more reflective, remarked on this feature:

A curiosity—it is of course not a defect—in the play's structure is the way woman dominates. Of course, the French girl does; it is her play. But that is not what is meant. There are seven men to five of the other sex, only two of whom matter, and the feminine side must talk fully three quarters of the words used. Also they have all the best lines[9].

Perhaps this quality of the play has something to do with its subsequent history: a play dominated by women is not likely to be a popular piece with the masculine vanities who dominate the commercial theatres. The *Bulletin* went on to say:

The play is a godsend to all such earnest and honest amateurs as the Turreteers, but that it is left to them is not much of a compliment to the commercial stage in this country.

Earnestness and honesty, to which the play has indeed been left until the present, do not preclude appalling conditions: the Turret Theatre, for instance, was a converted Council Chambers with a very narrow stage, where 'atmosphere' was interrupted continually by the roars of passing trams, and large props had been known to collapse in mid–scene[10].

The play has in fact been produced frequently by amateur groups, often without attention to the finer points such as author's royalties, especially once its original publication by Melbourne University Press in 1942 made the text readily available. In 1939 the New Theatre League in Sydney staged it, and the Tin Alley Players gave it a rehearsed reading at Melbourne University in 1957 under the direction of Keith Macartney.

The commercial stage in Australia kept its distance, although professional production abroad has been in sight several times[11].

However, the dismal tale of amateur interest and professional neglect is not the full story: *The Touch of Silk* has enjoyed a vigorous parallel existence as radio drama. The strange paradox by which radio kept Australian theatre alive during the 'thirties and 'forties, offering employment to actors, directors and writers, is an important chapter in Australian theatre history, which this play illustrates perfectly. From about 1928, the arrival of radio and talking films provided a new, large audience for dramatic writing throughout the West. In Australia, the film market was dominated from the beginning, as now, by imported works, but it was not quite so with 'the wireless'. A few stage plays indifferently adapted were being broadcast in the late 'twenties, but with the establishment of the ABC's Federal Department of Productions in 1936, dramatists were actively and effectively encouraged to write directly for radio. Adaptations of stage plays from that date showed more awareness of the demands of the new medium, and the radio play on both the ABC and commercial radio became a popular entertainment. An audience larger even that that commonly commanded by the commercial theatres was now able at least to hear Australian drama professionally produced[12].

There have been no less than fifteen separate productions of *The Touch of Silk* broadcast by the ABC[13]. The first production, at 3AR Melbourne in 1938, was produced by John Cairns, with Lucy Ahon from the original cast as Jeanne. The most often broadcast of the productions and the first to receive national relay was at 2FC Sydney, 1942, starring one of our best known and loved radio actresses, Neva Carr–Glynn, and produced by Charles Wheeler. Also of special note is the production at 7ZL Launceston in 1956, which was produced by Frank D. Clewlow, now retired from his position as Federal Programme Controller for the ABC.

It is not hard to find reasons for the play's popularity on radio. The central tension is bodied forth largely in aural terms: the difference in accent, the wind and the shutter in the second act, the final downpour and so on. Although the visual dimension would be missed in moments such as when Jeanne involuntarily touches the silk to her cheek at the very end of the play, the sense of surrounding space so necessary to convey the oppressive force of the drought is more easily achieved through sound effects than on the stage.

The fact remains that like so many Australian plays of its time that received high critical praise *The Touch of Silk*, now forty–five years old, has yet to receive a production which accords it the full amenities of the professional theatre. *The Time Is Not Yet Ripe* by Louis Esson languished sixty years between its first and second seasons, *The Bride of Gospel Place* nearly fifty; *Brumby Innes* by Katharine Susannah Prichard waited forty–five years to be produced at all; *The Touch of Silk*, more fortunate and up till now less so, is still waiting in the wings. Jonathan Hardy directed a workshop reading for the Melbourne Theatre Company in March 1974, so perhaps its time is about to come.

iii
The Text

There have been a number of adaptations of *The Touch of Silk*, not all of them by the hand of Betty Roland: at least two for radio, an updating to the mid–'fifties and an unauthorised Americanisation are the main ones[14]. There are only two versions, however, which can be regarded as authoritative texts for publication. The first is the text published by the Melbourne University Press in 1942, and reprinted in 1945 in a second edition, although the differences between the two editions are minor and in matters of style only. This publication, which

I shall call 1942, would seem to be the earliest extant text and is to all intents and purposes the corrected and definitive text of the original play. The other text, which exists only in manuscript, was written in 1973. and amounts to a substantial redrafting of the play. I shall call it A.

The revisions in A are designed to do away with what the author has come to see as the naiveties and crudities of the original work, to make it a more professional piece of writing and to bring it more into line with the prevailing tastes in theatre. Specifically, there are two kinds of alteration: major structural change and intensive local revision. The first act takes place eighteen months earlier than the second, in a time of prosperity and optimism, and as a result its mood contrasts strikingly with the desolation of Act Two; there is a second scene to the act in which David Ritchie and Nelly plight their troth at a dance; Constable Hughes is written out of the play altogether. We are given more information about the minor characters, so that the play's world is more substantial, more detailed. Clifford Osborne "fell in love with a bright–eyed senorita, but her father disapproved"; David Ritchie has persuaded his father to install electric light and other modernities in the store; the story of Mrs. Alexander Ritchie's elopement is given more fully; Jeanne is discussed much earlier in the piece; Mrs. Ryan, we learn, has nine children. The dialogue and stage directions throughout are so thoroughly rewritten that scarcely a single speech retains its original form. For instance, Dr. Wilson's first line becomes: "Every horse gets sold some time and every woman changes her mind." As a result of this extensive and intensive revision, the editor is presented with a simple choice between texts.

The case for accepting A is strong: in it the author, after decades of experience in writing for several media, and with an eye to the demands of professional production, refines, improves and polishes her youthful work, making it more craftsmanlike, more elegant, in a word more professional. Clearly it is this version by which she would prefer to be known in the present; and it is this version which a working theatrical director might well choose. But the editorial decision is more complicated. The play is being presented here as part of the neglected dramatic past of this country. Indeed, the fact that it has been possible for Betty Roland to revise her early play at such a distance from the original writing is perhaps symptomatic of the very phenomenon which the General Editor of this series seeks to counter, namely the absence of a sense of history: until quite recently, it seems, it has not been possible for an Australian play to be taken seriously unless it were recognisably contemporary in manner. Like the axe in the fable, the revised *Touch of Silk* is still more or less the same shape, still serves the same end, but is no longer of the same material—is it still the same thing? The original play is interesting largely for what it achieves in and through the highly contrived theatrical conventions of its day: the revised version, in attempting to render the play more 'realistic', shifts the grounds substantially. It seems to me that A is in fact a new play, and an untried new play at that.

For these reasons, and with the author's approval, the present volume presents the 1942 text with virtually no change, and a sampling of A in the appendix (see p. 92), to give an indication of the nature of the detailed revisions.

There are some instances in which the present text differs from 1942. Firstly, some very minor changes have been made to the stage directions to align the text with the National Theatre style. Secondly, there are two particulars in which A is preferred. The first concerns the rendition of Jeanne's dialogue, which is here spelled regularly, with no attempt to render her accent phonetically as 1942 does, thus:

No... no... no! Not if you offair me an 'undred pounds!
She is not for sale! And you will nevair make me say 'yes'.

(Compare p. 22)

This difference in style was accepted because the device tends to distract the reader, and as instruction to an actress is unnecessary, once the important general point has been made that Jeanne has a strong French accent. The second particular is similarly minor: 1942 places the action "in Australia ten years after the Armistice", and describes the setting for Act One as "any outback country store in Australia". The present reading (see p. 5, line 1) renders explicit the locality implied in the text. A is even more explicit, the opening stage direction beginning as follows:

It is Saturday morning in Quamby, a small town in the north–west of Victoria.

Other departures from 1942 are the following revisions made by the author in the proofs of the present volume:

p. 28 line 18: 1942 reads "as far as 'e can go?"

p. 37 line 10: 1942 reads "eat them when they are dead?"

p. 55 line 23: 1942 reads "someone else. You know".

Jonathan Shaw

Acknowledgements

I wish to acknowledge the courtesy of the staff of the Archives Department of the Australian Broadcasting Commission in Sydney, and of the La Trobe Librarian of the State Library of Victoria. I must also thank Miss Betty Roland for her invaluable and gracious assistance; and Miss Katharine Brisbane and especially the General Editor for their advice and encouragement.

The Touch of Silk

CHARACTERS:

MISS PATTERSON
CLIFFORD OSBORNE
ALEXANDER RITCHIE
MRS RYAN
JIM DAVIDSON
MRS DAVIDSON, Jim's mother
NELLY DAVIDSON, Jim's sister
DAVID RITCHIE, Ritchie's son
JEANNE, Jim's wife
DR WILSON
HARRY, the butcher's boy
CONSTABLE HUGHES

SETTING:

ACT ONE

The Millinery and Drapery Department of Ritchie's Store in a small
town in north–west Victoria. A Saturday morning in September.

ACT TWO

Scene One: Jeanne's farmhouse kitchen, three months later.

Scene Two: The same, eleven o'clock that night.

ACT THREE

The kitchen, next evening.

Act One

Saturday morning in a country store in north–west Victoria. In the centre of the wall at the back is a door marked 'Private'. Built on either side of this are several rows of shelves filled with a miscellaneous collection of drapery, ribbons, cardboard boxes, et cetera. There are also two counters at the back: on the left, one for the millinery department; on the right, one for the drapery. Along the right wall is a table, set out just far enough to allow an attendant to stand behind, and on this is arrayed a motley collection of voiles, prints and one or two lengths of gay–coloured silk. A second table is directly opposite, bearing a display of hats. From some rails suspended overhead, hang some casement curtains, belts, one or two jumpers on hangers, a length of lace, anything that might appeal to the taste of the class of customer that patronises the store. Two or three baskets of millinery trimmings, a long mirror and a few chairs complete the furnishings. Half reclining across the counter on the left is MISS PATTERSON, *of the millinery. She is slightly passé, slightly coy and very distinctly making a game stand against the total of the years behind her. She leans her chin in her hand and carries on an arch conversation with* CLIFFORD OSBORNE, *a clean–cut, rather attractive young man of about thirty–four. He is sorting and folding a pile of material that is lying on his counter and he answers with an air of good–natured tolerance, occasionally delighting her with a hint of gallantry. This comes more from kindness than inclination. He is good–natured, rather debonair, and has the gift of understanding the secret wishes of the human heart. He is sun–tanned and vigorous, not at all one's picture of the draper's assistant, and one feels again that air of tolerance as he plays the game of shop.*

MISS PATTERSON: Playing tennis this afternoon, Mr Osborne?

OSBORNE: No, not this afternoon. I'm going down to the river to have a bit of a fish.

MISS PATTERSON: Why don't you join our Club? We've got such a jolly crowd and have a dance once a month. You'll meet all the nice people there.

OSBORNE: Oh, I'm going to join all right. I haven't had much time to think about things like that yet. It takes a little time to get settled down again, you know.

MISS PATTERSON: But you've been here five weeks and I've asked you to come with me several times.

OSBORNE: Well, you ask me to come again next Saturday and I'll be there.

MISS PATTERSON: Will you? That's a promise now?

OSBORNE: That's a promise.

MISS PATTERSON: Oh, that's fine. I'm sure you'll like all the crowd. Such a lot have been asking why you haven't been along.

OSBORNE: To tell the truth, it seems so funny to be back here again. I've just been fooling round, going to all the old places I used to know when I was a kid.

MISS PATTERSON: And what does this place seem like, now that you have come back?

OSBORNE: Not half so big or so important.

MISS PATTERSON: [*sighing enviously*] You must have seen some wonderful places when you were away.

OSBORNE: Yes… they were wonderful… some of them. But there's a sort of sameness about places after a while.

MISS PATTERSON: Mr Osborne… I believe you're *blasé*!

OSBORNE: [*amused*] Well, perhaps I am… when it comes to getting a kick out of knocking round the world in a tramp steamer.

MISS PATTERSON: But it all seems so romantic… going to the War when you were so young and then the sea. I can't imagine how you can settle down to work in a place like this. It must seem awfully tame.

OSBORNE: Not at all, Miss Patterson. It's a novelty and, after all, that's what everybody is after when they go for a trip round the world, isn't it?

MISS PATTERSON: I suppose so, but if you'd been working here for eleven years like I have, I guess some of the novelty would have about worn off.

OSBORNE: Well, for my part, I've never stuck to a job for more than two months in my life, so I'm going to see if I can't work up a bit of a novelty by hanging on to this one.

MISS PATTERSON: Oh… you are terrible!

During OSBORNE*'s last lines she has straightened up and made a pretence at doing some work. The reason for this is apparent when* ALEXANDER RITCHIE, *the owner of the store, comes in. He is a hard, grey Scot, a man of his word, scrupulously honest, but as unsparing to others as he is to himself.*

RITCHIE: [*crossing towards* OSBORNE] Those other cases are open now; you can go and bring some of the things in.

OSBORNE: Shall I bring them in here?

RITCHIE: You'd better do so for the time being. You'll be wanting some of them as samples to take out with you on Monday. Let me have a look at them before you go.

OSBORNE: Very well, Mr Ritchie.

He finishes stacking the materials and goes out through the archway at left.

RITCHIE: Did you get the invoices for that new lot of stuff, Miss Patterson?

MISS PATTERSON: Yes, Mr Ritchie. I put them on the table in your office.

RITCHIE: Oh… thank you.

He looks at the materials OSBORNE *has been sorting.* MRS RYAN *comes bustling in. She is a thin, arid shrimp of a woman, shrill of voice and hard of hand, quick–eyed and sharp–tongued.*

MRS RYAN: 'Ullo, Stella. You're looking well. Got a bit fat since I seen yer last, haven't yer?

MISS PATTERSON: Oh, don't say that, Mrs Ryan, and me thinking I was getting quite slim.

MRS RYAN: Laws… what d'yer want t'do that for? It's only them silly bits of girls with their eye on some man that bothers about that sort of thing.

RITCHIE *looks up and is caught by her roving eye.*

Good day, Mr Ritchie.

RITCHIE: Good day, Mrs Ryan. How are you?

MRS RYAN: Oh… I'm nicely, thank you. Can't say I ever felt better.

RITCHIE: That's good.

He resumes his examination of the materials.

MRS RYAN: Where's that young man gone to? I was wanting some stuff.

MISS PATTERSON: He won't be long, Mrs Ryan. He just went out to get some things for Mr Ritchie.

MRS RYAN: Oh, I see. [*Touching some of the hats*] These things are new, ain't they?

MISS PATTERSON: Yes, those are our new season's stock. How do you like this?

> MRS RYAN *plumps down her suitcase and parcels and proceeds to examine the hats.* JIM DAVIDSON *comes in. He hesitates at the sight of the women but* MISS PATTERSON *smiles brightly at him and puts him at his ease. He is a man of thirty–odd, but ill health and overstrain have prematurely greyed his hair and carved deep lines around his mouth and nostrils. There is an air of frailty about his hands and the long, nervous fingers twist his hat as he slowly crosses to where* RITCHIE *is and comes to a halt beside him.*

JIM: Good day, Mr Ritchie.

RITCHIE: [*turning around*] Oh… good day, Jim. How are you?

JIM: I'm all right, Mr Ritchie.

> *There is a strained pause while* JIM *shifts uncomfortably on his feet.*

I was wanting to have a talk to you about things, Mr Ritchie.

RITCHIE: Oh, yes. What is it, Jim?

JIM: Well… it's about that money, Mr Ritchie.

RITCHIE: Yes?

> *He is perfectly non–committal and turns to pick up a ledger from the counter.* JIM *is painfully nervous and moistens his dry lips.*

JIM: I was wondering if you… if it was possible for you to give me a little more time?

> RITCHIE *makes no reply but his brow darkens a little and he draws down his lips.*

[*Jerkily*] You see… I didn't get what I figured for those sheep. Everything being so dry has made the price come down…

RITCHIE: How many did you sell?

JIM: Three hundred.

RITCHIE: And what did you get?

JIM: Twelve shillings.

RITCHIE: Hum!

JIM: You see… those are some of the sheep I bought with the money I got from you at the beginning of the year. I paid over a pound for some of them.

RITCHIE: And you sold at twelve shillings. That doesn't seem like good business to me, Jim.

JIM: I know, Mr Ritchie, and I never would have done it if it hadn't have been that I haven't got the grass to feed them.

RITCHIE: How many are you carrying to the acre?

JIM: Two.

RITCHIE: Two! You're asking for bother. The country round here is never safe for two.

JIM: [*with a hint of desperation*] But I've done it before, so has everybody else, and I would have been all right this time if only we'd got the rain.

RITCHIE: That's a chance you always take when you overstock. What are you going to do if a drought hits you?

JIM: I've thought of that and that's what I want to see you about. I've got an uncle down in Gippsland, Mr Ritchie, and he can give me grazing for about seven or eight hundred, if I like to send them down there.

RITCHIE: Gippsland! That's a long way to send stock.

JIM: I can manage it, Mr Ritchie, if you let me have a little more time to meet my payments to you.

> JIM's *fortune hangs in the balance and he watches anxiously as* RITCHIE *looks down at the floor.*

RITCHIE: It amounts to this. You want me to let you keep the money you've got from the sale of those sheep in order to pay for the transport of the others to Gippsland?

JIM: It's my only chance of pulling out, Mr Ritchie.

RITCHIE: But only a chance.

JIM: It's going to avoid what will happen if we don't get rain. I can't face a drought, overstocked like I am.

RITCHIE: That's all very well, but will you ever get your money back on them? Even if you do send them away?

JIM: What else can I do? I'm short of feed now and in another month or two they'll be dying like flies.

RITCHIE: If I were you, I'd sell and cut my losses.

JIM: I can't afford to sell at half the price I gave for them. They're bought on borrowed money. Good God!... You should know that.

> JIM's *voice rises in his anxiety.* RITCHIE *looks across the shop and sees that the eyes of the two women are fixed curiously on them.*

RITCHIE: We can't talk here. Come into my office.

JIM: [*calming down*] I'll have to go out and tell Ma and Nelly. I was to meet them here.

RITCHIE: All right. You'll find me in there when you come back.

> *He turns and goes through the door marked 'Private'.* JIM *walks out through the archway without a glance in the direction of* MISS PATTERSON *and* MRS RYAN. *They exchange knowing glances.*

MRS RYAN: I heard he was in trouble.

MISS PATTERSON: Poor chap. He's looking real bad, isn't he?

MRS RYAN: We'll all be feeling the pinch soon, I expect, but it's no good of meeting trouble half–way, I says. [*Getting up and going over to the drapery counter*] This some new stuff, too?

MISS PATTERSON: Yes, they're just in. They're samples Mr Osborne is taking out with him on Monday. Did you know he was taking over the country round from Mr Fletcher?

MRS RYAN: Go on, is he? Well, I didn't know that. That's a rise for him, ain't it?

MISS PATTERSON: Yes, it is, really, but he's a good salesman... he's got a sort of a way with him.

MRS RYAN: Oh... I know that all right. I bet business has gone up in this department since he got a job here.

> OSBORNE *comes breezily in, laden with rolls of material. He goes behind the counter, dumps them down and smiles at* MRS RYAN. *The lady is not by any means proof against his charm and she beams back.*

OSBORNE: Good–morning, Mrs Ryan. Have I kept you waiting?

MRS RYAN: Oh, no… not for long. I've been talking to Miss Patterson here.

OSBORNE: [*gallantly*] Then I'm not going to say I'm sorry.

> *He smiles broadly at them both. In their drab lives he is something of a thrill and his easy flattery delights them.*

What can I do for you?

MRS RYAN: Well, I was thinking I would like to have a look at some of the summer stuffs. It'll soon be getting warm now.

OSBORNE: We've got a fine lot of new materials in, Mrs Ryan; we've just been opening them up today. But why don't you wait until I'm out your way next week and let me call out and show them to you in your own home?

MRS RYAN: Oh, I don't know. I might as well have a look at them now.

OSBORNE: But you won't be able to see the full range of our stock. This is only a very poor sample of what we will have.

MRS RYAN: [*hesitating*] Perhaps it might be just as well…

OSBORNE: Just as you like, of course… but if you're wanting anything for the girls…

MRS RYAN: Oh, yes… Mary and Grace'll have to have something. We're going down to the Show this year.

> *She preens herself as she announces this bit of social splendour.*

OSBORNE: Are you now? That's fine. Well, some of the things that I will have to show you when I come out will be just as good as anything you will see in Melbourne. Just wait a minute till I bring in some of the voiles I saw outside.

MRS RYAN: Good–oh!

> *She settles herself back for a pleasant ten minutes as* OSBORNE *hurries out.*

MISS PATTERSON: He's looking well, isn't he?

MRS RYAN: He is that. He always was a nice boy, Cliff. Pity he's always been such a wandering sort of fellow. He might have done some good otherwise.

MISS PATTERSON: Well, you don't know. Perhaps he might turn over a new leaf and settle down now.

> *Enter* MRS DAVIDSON, JIM *and* NELLY. MRS DAVIDSON *is almost*

a counterpart of MRS RYAN. NELLY *is about twenty. She has a certain amount of beauty in a fair and heavy way. It is obvious that the hopes of the family are fixed on her as she is dressed rather attractively and far more expensively than her shabby and toil–worn mother. She has an air of superior tolerance for her elders and maintains this all through the scene.* JIM *takes no part in the noisy greetings that follow their entry. His mind is fixed on the man who sits behind the door marked 'Private'.*

MRS DAVIDSON: There you are, Mrs Ryan. I seen your husband outside and he told me you were in here somewhere.

MRS RYAN: Well, I didn't expect to see you in here this morning.

MRS DAVIDSON: Jim had to come in on business, so Nelly and I thought we might as well come in too. It must be six weeks since I was last in town.

JIM: I'll go now, Ma. You've got some things to do, haven't you?

MRS DAVIDSON: Yes, don't you bother about us. Nelly and I'll do what we have to and then we'll go and sit in the trap.

JIM: Right–oh! I won't be more than half an hour.

He goes up to the door, knocks and passes through.

MRS DAVIDSON: Poor Jim… he's nervous.

She glances after him, her face lined with anxiety.

MRS RYAN: I thought he wasn't looking well. I haven't seen him look that way since he first came back from the War.

MRS DAVIDSON: For the Lord's sake don't let him hear you say that. If there's anything that Jim can't stand it's to be reminded of how he was then. He nearly bit me head off for saying something like you did the other day. Why, hullo, Stella! I didn't see you over there.

MISS PATTERSON: Good–morning, Mrs Davidson… Nelly!

NELLY, *who has been idly looking about the shop, looks up at the greeting and smiles briefly back. She considers the somewhat drab little milliner altogether out of her class and wastes no time on useless formalities.*

MRS DAVIDSON: You're just the one I want to see, Stella. I brought that old straw hat of mine in to see what you would do with it. Give it to me, Nelly.

NELLY *comes out of her preoccupation sufficiently to hand over the paper bag she carries. Out of this is produced the hat. It is of no particular shape, no particular colour.*

MRS RYAN: That's been a good hat!

MRS DAVIDSON: Too right, it has! I've had three seasons' wear out of it and I guess I'll get another.

MISS PATTERSON: I always liked you in that hat, Mrs Davidson.

MRS DAVIDSON: Well, I must say I'm getting a bit tired of it myself… still some fresh trimmings should brighten it up.

MISS PATTERSON: You're not going to have a new one this spring, Mrs Davidson?

MRS DAVIDSON: No… I'm going to wait until we see how things are going. What do you think would go on it, Stella?

MISS PATTERSON: Let me see… it had a feather before I put on that ribbon, didn't it?

MRS RYAN: I like something bright myself, especially as it's not a new hat.

MISS PATTERSON: Yes, I was thinking that…

OSBORNE *comes in with the voiles.*

MRS DAVIDSON: Well, I'm blessed if it isn't Cliff Osborne!

Down goes the hat and she crosses the stage to grasp his hand.

You remember me? Mrs Davidson… Jim's mother.

OSBORNE: You bet I do… How are you? It's old times to see you again.

MRS DAVIDSON: Too right it is! What are you doing back here? I thought you'd gone for good.

MRS RYAN: Haven't you seen him before?

MRS DAVIDSON: No, I told you it's been weeks since I was in here last. I'd heard you was back, but I had no idea you were in here.

OSBORNE: Always trust the bad penny to turn up again.

MRS DAVIDSON: Well, you've been long enough about it, young man. Here, Nelly… you remember Cliff, don't you?

NELLY *has come out of her trance and has been surreptitiously preening herself with the aid of the mirror in her handbag.* MRS DAVIDSON *draws her forward.*

OSBORNE: Is this Nelly? Well I never! You've grown some since I saw you last. Are you as shy now as you were then, Nelly?

NELLY *laughs non–committally and does not answer.*

MRS DAVIDSON: Never know her to be the same girl, would you?

NELLY *flounces away from the too–fond mother and* MRS DAVIDSON *turns to* MISS PATTERSON *and* MRS RYAN.

Fancy this black sheep turning up again.

MISS PATTERSON: [*primly*] Everybody was very surprised to see Mr Osborne again.

MRS RYAN: I should think so. The last we heard of him he was working in a mine in Peru... that was about two years ago... and the next thing, he turns up here, as large as life.

OSBORNE: No place like home, Mrs Ryan.

MRS RYAN: Well, you're the one should know; you've tried everywhere else. [*Turning back to the counter*] Are these the stuffs you was telling me about?

OSBORNE: These are the ones. Aren't they nice?

MRS RYAN: [*to* MRS DAVIDSON] I'll have a look at these while you're fixing up about your hat, Mrs Davidson, and then perhaps we can have a bit of dinner together before we go home.

MRS DAVIDSON: That'll suit me fine.

NELLY *joins* MRS RYAN *at the drapery counter while her mother devotes her attention to* MISS PATTERSON.

MISS PATTERSON: How do you think some of these flowers would do, Mrs Davidson?

They both bend over a basket of trimmings.

MRS DAVIDSON: [*producing a bunch of extremely pink roses*] These ain't too bad.

MISS PATTERSON: Yes... [*with a bunch of scarlet poppies*] or what about these?

MRS DAVIDSON: No, I don't care for red in the hot weather.

They rummage in the basket once again.

Let's have a try at those roses. I rather fancy them, somehow.

MISS PATTERSON: Oh, they're real pretty, and just new in too. Shall I put them in the hat for you so's you can try it on?

MRS DAVIDSON: That's a good idea. You might as well.

She hands across the hat and settles back in her chair.

How's that boil your husband had, Mrs Ryan?

MRS RYAN: It's been something cruel. Do you know I've had to be up with hot water for two nights and he hasn't sat down to a meal for days.

MRS DAVIDSON: Go on! That's terrible, ain't it? I've had them lots of times but never there.

MISS PATTERSON: Boils are horrid things.

MRS DAVIDSON: It seems to me there's always something in this life to keep us from being happy! I wonder how poor Jim is getting on?

MISS PATTERSON: [*busy with the hat*] I suppose you'll be feeling anxious till you know.

MRS DAVIDSON: Anxious is right. It's terrible the way that old skinflint holds so many of us in the hollow of his hand, as the saying is.

MISS PATTERSON: And yet, the farmers couldn't get on without the credit he gives them.

MRS DAVIDSON: I don't know so much about that. Perhaps if he didn't give them credit like he does, they wouldn't go getting in so deep. Look at Jim; he would never have bought this other place if Ritchie hadn't helped him put up the money.

MISS PATTERSON: But then, with any luck, Jim will pay it off and he'll have a nice lot of property then.

MRS DAVIDSON: With any luck, yes! But what about if we don't get the rain? Ritchie holds the deeds and he can sell up every bit of land we own. I don't like it, and I tell you straight.

MISS PATTERSON: He'll never do a thing like that. He'll give Jim time.

MRS DAVIDSON: Oh, I don't know so much about that.

> MISS PATTERSON *snaps the thread of cotton with her teeth and hands the hat across.*

MISS PATTERSON: Will you try this on now? I've only fastened the flowers in loosely.

> MRS DAVIDSON *stands up and puts on the hat in front of the mirror. The effect is distinctly festive.*

MRS DAVIDSON: Well, that ain't too bad. What do you say, Nelly?

NELLY: It's all right.

MRS DAVIDSON: All right! Is that all you've got to say? You'd think she hadn't a tongue in her head, Mrs Ryan, to hear her now, but, my word, you should see the difference when young David Ritchie comes round.

NELLY: Oh, Ma! Do be quiet!

MRS RYAN: I've heard rumours of a fine smart motor car coming down our way lately.

MRS DAVIDSON: You'll be hearing more than rumours one of these days, I shouldn't be surprised.

NELLY: [*not displeased and with a sidelong glance at* OSBORNE] Ma! Do stop it!

MRS DAVIDSON: There's stranger things have happened before today.

MRS RYAN: Well, he's a nice boy and I think you're a lucky girl, Nelly.

OSBORNE: What's this, Nelly?

NELLY: It's nothing at all. I don't know what they're talking about.

MRS DAVIDSON: No more do I… but I've a fair idea. What do you think of this hat, Mrs Ryan?

MRS RYAN: I think it's real nice.

MRS DAVIDSON: All right, I suppose I may as well have these roses then. I'll leave it here and get you to send it out one day next week, Stella.

> MRS RYAN *exchanges a few words with* OSBORNE *and leaves his counter.* NELLY *has already crossed to the other part of the shop.* OSBORNE *picks up his book and commences to go out, almost colliding with a young man who comes hurrying in. He is* DAVID RITCHIE, NELLY*'s lover, a clean–cut, likeable boy, reasonably good–looking.*

DAVID: Sorry, old man!

OSBORNE: That's all right.

> *He goes out.*

DAVID: Hello, Nelly. I've been hunting all over the town for you. Hello, Mrs Davidson… Mrs Ryan!

MRS DAVIDSON & MRS RYAN: }Hello, David… Hello, Dave!

DAVID: Wherever did you get yourself to, Nelly?

He is obviously in love with her, and goes up and takes her arm.

NELLY: I've been with Ma, just in the shops.

DAVID: Well, I've been after you for the last hour. I want you to come to a dance at Wentworth to–night... can you?

They both look across at MRS DAVIDSON.

MRS DAVIDSON: Yes, that's right... you go along, Nell.

DAVID: Good–oh! I'm driving up this afternoon. We'll call in at your place on the way and you can pick up some clothes.

NELLY: Oh, that'll be lovely.

Her heaviness has left her. She has become youthful and animated.

DAVID: Come on then. We'll go and get something to eat. You don't mind if I run away with her now, do you, Mrs Davidson?

MRS DAVIDSON: [*fondly*] No, you two get off and have as good a time as you can. I'll manage all right.

NELLY: Can you take all these things, Ma?

MRS DAVIDSON: Of course I can. Jim'll be out in a minute and he'll give me a hand.

NELLY: All right then. Good–bye, Mrs Ryan... good–bye, Miss Patterson.

They all call out 'Good–bye', 'So long', and MRS RYAN, *last of all, 'Have a good time', as* DAVID *and* NELLY *go.*

MRS RYAN: Well, Nelly's a lucky girl.

MRS DAVIDSON: Yes, she is that. It's a great thing for a girl to have a nice young chap like Dave, [*with a glance about the store*] and everything so comfortable, too.

MRS RYAN: [*jerking her head towards the office*] The old man said anything about it yet?

MRS DAVIDSON: No, he never takes any notice of what the boy does. Gives him all the money he wants and then forgets him.

MRS RYAN: He's a queer stick, is Ritchie. Mind you... [*coming across to speak with lowered voice*] he didn't use to be like that. It's only since he had that trouble with his wife.

MISS PATTERSON: Oh, you're right there, Mrs Ryan. I'll never forget the way he looked after... she first went away. He's never been really what you'd call... nice since.

MRS RYAN: Well, all I can say is that he's a lucky man to be getting such a fine, steady girl as Nelly for his son. His own wasn't that kind at all. Too pretty... too fond of a good time!

MRS DAVIDSON: I should say so. Any man'd be lucky to get my Nell, let alone Ritchie. Why, I remember him when he first come out from the old country. As poor a specimen as you'd ever see. And look at him now, the biggest man in the town, and worth thousands.

MRS RYAN: That's true. Australia's been pretty good to him, considering he thought he was coming out here to die in a few months.

Her eye strays through the archway and she waves her hand and calls out.

All right. Coming. [*To* MRS DAVIDSON] There's Ryan now. I'll have to get out to him. Are you coming now or will we meet later?

MRS DAVIDSON: I'll wait a while. I've got to meet Jan here.

MRS RYAN: All right then. We'll see you up at the Commercial. [*Gathering up her parcels*] Ta–ta, for the present, then. Ta–ta, Stella.

MISS PATTERSON: Good–bye, Mrs Ryan.

MRS DAVIDSON: Ta–ta!

Exit MRS RYAN.

I wonder how the time's getting on?

MISS PATTERSON: It's a quarter to one, Mrs Davidson.

MRS DAVIDSON: A quarter to one! I wonder what's keeping that Jan? She should have been here ages ago. Did you see her anywhere about?

MISS PATTERSON: She hasn't been in here this morning.

MRS DAVIDSON: Then where's she got herself to? I never in my life knew anyone with less idea of time than that girl.

MISS PATTERSON: Something must have delayed her, surely.

MRS DAVIDSON: She only had to go and see Dr Wilson, and Jim left her there over an hour ago.

MISS PATTERSON: Hasn't she been well?

MRS DAVIDSON: Only the outcome of that last bit of trouble of hers. But it strikes me there's only one thing the matter with her and that's discontent.

MISS PATTERSON: She doesn't seem very happy out here, does she?

MRS DAVIDSON: And more shame to her! What's she got to be unhappy about, I'd like to know, with a good husband like Jim, a home of her own and nothing to want for? More than she'd have ever got where she came from!

MISS PATTERSON: But I always think it's hard on a girl to come to a strange country and not to know a single soul.

MRS DAVIDSON: I can understand her being a bit homesick and strange at first, but after ten years! She's had plenty of time to settle down and get used to things.

MISS PATTERSON: It's a pity she hasn't been able to have any children.

MRS DAVIDSON: [*acidly*] It's more than a pity, I think. All these misses seem a funny thing to me. I never had such a thing in my life and I worked every bit as hard as she did. There's more in that than meets the eye.

MISS PATTERSON: You mean…

MRS DAVIDSON: I don't think she means to have any at all.

MISS PATTERSON: [*electrified*] Oh… surely!

MRS DAVIDSON: These French girls know a thing or two about matters of that kind, take it from me! Not as I'd care to have either her or Jim know as I'd said it, mind.

MISS PATTERSON: Oh, no, of course not. But you could hardly think that of her somehow. She seems such a nice little thing. I can't understand how it is she never seems to settle down and make any friends.

MRS DAVIDSON: And is that to be wondered at? It's first impressions that count and will I ever forget the way that girl carried on when she first came out? I tell you, without a word of a lie, I never seen a bunch of men, and all going off into fits of laughter, but I used to go hot and cold all over for fear I'd find that Jan in the middle of them, and saying the most awful things!

MISS PATTERSON: But she never meant to say them. It was just that she didn't know English very well.

MRS DAVIDSON: That is as maybe, but it seemed a funny thing to me, and to lots of others that I could name too, that the mistakes she made was always on the fast side!

MISS PATTERSON: Well, I must say, I always liked her. She seemed such a gay little thing when she first came out.

MRS DAVIDSON: Gay's right.

MISS PATTERSON: Anyhow, she's quieted down a lot since then.

MRS DAVIDSON: Oh yes... on top. She soon found out that you can't do that sort of thing out here and keep your good name, but I fancy there's not much change underneath somehow...

Just at this moment JEANNE's *voice, high–pitched, clear and full of laughter, comes clearly from the other portion of the shop. Both women turn to look as she comes in. She is small, chic and dainty, dressed in a neat black frock, plain almost to a point of severity, but having withal that indescribable air of smartness that seems to be the special heritage of the Frenchwoman. With her is* DR WILSON, *stout, genial and middle–aged. Long experience and many trials have mellowed him into a kindly philosopher with a shrewd understanding of the spiritual, as well as the physical, ills of his struggling country practice. For* JEANNE *he has a special sympathy and an unvoiced pity. At present they are sharing a joke and come in laughing together.*

JEANNE: No... no... no! Not if you offer me an 'undred pounds! She is not for sale! And you will never make me say yes.

WILSON: Nonsense! Every horse is born to be sold and every woman to be persuaded.

JEANNE: Not this 'orse... not this woman! I would not sell Colette, not if I starve. It is 'opeless, monsieur doctor, you 'ad better give it up!

MRS DAVIDSON: [*putting a stop to this nonsense*] There you are, Jan. I've been waiting here for you for ages.

A light seems to die in JEANNE *and she makes a little apologetic gesture.*

WILSON: I'm the culprit, Mrs Davidson. I've been trying to persuade her to sell me that mare of hers, but not a bit of good can I get out of her.

MRS DAVIDSON: Oh, you'll never get Jan to sell you Colette. She makes as much fuss over that horse as if it was a child.

JEANNE: And why not? I love 'er as much.

MRS DAVIDSON: Well, it's a pity you can't find something better to waste your affections on than that.

WILSON: [*changing the subject*] How are you, anyway, Mrs Davidson?

People like you are no good to a poor, struggling country doctor; you're far too healthy.

MRS DAVIDSON: Well, I can't complain, doctor.

WILSON: I should think you couldn't. I'd give a hundred pounds to be as fit as you are, and you're getting younger every time I see you.

MRS DAVIDSON: Now, doctor, it's always you with the blarney.

WILSON: Not a bit of it. Look at yourself in the mirror there and see if it's one word of a lie I'm telling you. What do you say, Miss Patterson?

MISS PATTERSON: I think Mrs Davidson is looking splendid, especially in this hat with the new roses.

> *She holds it aloft in triumph. Both the doctor and* JEANNE *look slightly aghast. There is a moment of silence.*

WILSON: It certainly is a grand hat.

JEANNE: Oh… Maman… are you going to 'ave those roses in your 'at?

MRS DAVIDSON: Yes, I am.

JEANNE: [*weakly*] Oh… are you?

MRS DAVIDSON: Why? Don't you like them?

JEANNE: Yes, they are very nice roses… but do you really like them in that 'at?

> *In spite of herself this last comes out. She is anxious to avoid giving offence, but her good taste cannot let the garish flowers pass unprotested.*

MRS DAVIDSON: What's the matter with them?

WILSON: [*scenting a storm*] There's nothing the matter with them, Mrs Davidson. They're just the very thing and don't you take any notice of what anybody says.

MRS DAVIDSON: But I want to know what Jan means.

JEANNE: I did not mean anything, Maman!

MRS DAVIDSON: But you think there's something wrong?

MISS PATTERSON: [*loftily*] Those flowers are very suitable for that type of hat.

JEANNE: For that type of 'at… maybe… but just right for Mrs Davidson, do you think? See… I show you what I mean.

> *With one of her swift movements she takes up a pair of scissors*

and has the offending roses out of the hat before any of them are well aware of her intention.

Now wait… I show you something. There are lots of pretty things in 'ere. Look! The very thing!

She has been searching through the basket of trimmings and finds a simple feather mount. She takes some pins, fastens it in, and comes forward to where MRS DAVIDSON *and* MISS PATTERSON *are watching her, almost open–mouthed.*

Just a little twist 'ere and there and… see… is it not smart?

MRS DAVIDSON *takes it with an air of silent wrath, turns to the mirror and jerks it on to her head.*

What do you think, doctor?

WILSON: Well, it's hard to say; it looks fine both ways.

MRS DAVIDSON: Well, I must say! I don't want those things in me hat.

JEANNE: But, Maman, they are so smart… and so becoming. See… [*pulling it to a different angle*] don't you like it now?

MRS DAVIDSON: I can't say as I do. It don't seem the same hat at all.

MISS PATTERSON: Of course it is a totally different class of hat with that style of trimming.

She is not over–pleased at JEANNE's *encroachment on her preserves.*

JEANNE: Of course! See, these roses, they are meant to be worn like this.

She places them at the shoulder of her dress.

MRS DAVIDSON: I suppose what you really mean is that I'm too old for that sort of thing. Oh well, that ends it then.

She jerks off the hat, puts it down and commences to tug on her other one.

MISS PATTERSON: Oh, Mrs Davidson!

JEANNE: No… no! I did not mean it that way at all. I only mean that they were not the very nicest things that you could 'ave.

WILSON: Now, Mrs Davidson, you put that hat on again and let us have a good look at it.

MRS DAVIDSON: [*enjoying her offence*] No, you've gone and got me clean off it now, between the lot of you. I'd made up me mind for one thing and then you go and change it round until I don't know what I want.

JEANNE: But look… look… I can put them back again. It will not take a minute.

She takes out the offending feathers and returns the roses.

MRS DAVIDSON: No, I haven't time today. I've been keeping Mrs Ryan waiting as it is. Some other time, Stella.

She commences to gather up her parcels.

JEANNE: [*following her*] Oh, please… please… don't misunderstand!

MRS DAVIDSON: Oh no… you're probably quite right. I must have looked a guy in pink roses! Good–bye, doctor. Call in and have a cup of tea if you're out our way.

WILSON: That I will, Mrs Davidson. Here, let me help you with those parcels.

MRS DAVIDSON: Thank you, doctor, that's kind of you. [*Handing him some of her packages*] Good–bye, Stella. I'm sure I'm sorry for all the trouble you've been put to, but I'll call some other day.

MISS PATTERSON: That's all right, Mrs Davidson. Perhaps we'll have something you will like better then.

MRS DAVIDSON: [*to* JEANNE] You'll be waiting here for Jim, I suppose?

JEANNE: 'As Jim not finished yet?

MRS DAVIDSON: I should think not. You can't do business like Jim's in five minutes. Goodness knows how long he will be.

JEANNE: Well, I will wait 'ere.

MRS DAVIDSON: You'll find me down at the Commercial Hotel when you're ready. I'm having dinner there with Mrs Ryan.

OSBORNE *comes in.*

Ta–ta, Cliff. I suppose we'll be seeing you before long?

OSBORNE: Yes, I'll be coming out your way next week.

MRS DAVIDSON: Well, see you call in.

OSBORNE: I'll be coming in all right.

MRS DAVIDSON: Ta–ta, Stella.

She goes through the archway. JEANNE *is left standing alone on the other side of the shop. She is in high disfavour and no word is spoken to her until the doctor turns just as he is about to follow* MRS DAVIDSON.

WILSON: And I'm coming out to see about that mare!

JEANNE *does not reply but shakes her head slowly, her smile a bit subdued and wistful. There is a little lull after they have gone out.* MISS PATTERSON *commences to put away some of the hats.* JEANNE *is about to speak to her but she turns away, whether deliberately or not is hard to tell.* JEANNE *shrugs her shoulders and walks to the other side of the shop, pausing to look at various things as she passes.* OSBORNE *is behind his counter and raises his eyes to look at her as she comes to a halt before a length of bright–coloured silk.*

OSBORNE: That's a nice piece of stuff.

JEANNE: It is beautiful.

She lifts a corner of it to her cheek.

OSBORNE: Nice and soft, isn't it?

JEANNE: Wonderful!

OSBORNE: That is some of our new spring stuff. You should come in on Monday and see it on show.

JEANNE: Your pretty things will all be sold before I come 'ere again.

OSBORNE: You don't come in very often?

JEANNE: Sometimes not for weeks and weeks.

OSBORNE: Don't you really? But you don't live so very far out.

JEANNE: Ten mile. It is quite far enough.

OSBORNE: Yes, it's a good way, but all the more reason for coming in here as often as you can.

JEANNE: And for what does one come in 'ere, monsieur?

OSBORNE: [*rather nonplussed*] Well… it makes a kind of a break, doesn't it? Don't you find it very lonely out there?

JEANNE: Sometime… yes… but not so bad… as once.

OSBORNE: You're French, aren't you?

JEANNE: [*as though admitting to a crime*] Yes… I am a French girl!

OSBORNE: What part do you come from?

JEANNE: Paree… Paris.

OSBORNE: Paris, do you? I know Paris fairly well. I was there just this time last year.

JEANNE: In Paree? Last year? But... 'ow marvellous!

Her impulse is to touch him, as one would some sacred thing.

OSBORNE: It's a far cry from here to Paris, isn't it?

JEANNE: Far? Oh... monsieur!

She seats herself on the chair in front of him.

OSBORNE: How long have you been out here?

JEANNE: With this year, it is ten years.

OSBORNE: Ten years!

JEANNE: Ten years.

OSBORNE: Time enough to forget a little bit about it, I suppose?

JEANNE: Forget? I would never forget in *twenty* years! Tell me, is it just the same?

OSBORNE: Pretty much, I should think. Different people, a few new places, but the same old life as ever.

JEANNE: I suppose so. Tell me, monsieur, where 'ave you been in Paree?

OSBORNE: Well... I've been to most of the places people do go. The Louvre, the Bois de Boulogne... Sacré Coeur... the Folies Bergères...

JEANNE: *And* Le Moulin Rouge! Monsieur, you 'ave no need to tell me that. Was there ever yet the stranger come to Paree that did not go there as fast as 'e can? 'E think that 'e 'ave seen all the wicked sights of Paree when 'e 'ave seen those naked ladies there.

MISS PATTERSON *stands spell–bound, but neither of them are aware of her presence.*

OSBORNE: You think there's more in Paris than meets the eye, then?

JEANNE: Ah... that is all so common... it is vulgar! That is not Paree at all. It is like your wax–works... something to see, that is all. For me, I 'ave always pity for those poor girls in there. If a woman 'ave to take off all her clothes to make the people look... she 'ave not got very much... for the next time... 'as she?

OSBORNE: No... perhaps not.

JEANNE: Of course not, I know it. But, tell me, monsieur, were you ever at La Faire de Neuilly, where all the real Parisians go, to see some fun and 'ave a laugh? Where a girl would get insulted… quick… if she go in alone?

OSBORNE: Yes, I've been there. And La Faire du Trône?

JEANNE: And Bullier, where the students go, and all the pretty little cocottes?

OSBORNE: And the Bal Tabarin and Moulin de la Jalette…

Their excitement is rising.

JEANNE: Oui… oui… and Coucou à Montmartre with its funny little tables and the kerosene lamps that don't give too much light!

OSBORNE: And had fried fish at Boulogne sur Seine?

JEANNE: Oh… monsieur! You almost make me die of longing. Do you know I 'ad forgotten. Just to think I 'ad forgotten, when I love it all so much. Oh… those lovely little fish… *friture*… You do not know how wonderful it is to 'ear of all those things again.

OSBORNE: Is it?

JEANNE: Oh, it is, indeed. There is no–one 'ere that know those places. Why… it gives me pain… in 'ere… just to hear the names again.

She places a hand over her heart.

OSBORNE: You miss the old life so much?

JEANNE: [*rising to her feet*] Can you ask?

She gives one of her expressive gestures that seems to embrace the drab country store, the dull outlook of those with whom she is forced to associate, and holds them up in contrast with the great world from which she has come.

OSBORNE: I know what you mean. I felt it all, even when I was a kid and had never been out of the place. That is why I chucked it and got away.

JEANNE: And now… you 'ave come back?

OSBORNE: God knows what for. I often wonder what on earth possessed me.

JEANNE: It was the call of your own. And, just think, if this place, this ugly little place, can bring you back, what must it be like for me, who 'ave come from Paree?

OSBORNE: [*laughing, his patriotism aroused*] Oh, come… This isn't such a bad sort of town. We've got a population of five thousand…

a fire brigade... and an electric light plant... What more do you
want?

JEANNE: Ah... you know what I mean.

OSBORNE: I do. It must be pretty stiff for you sometimes.

JEANNE: Not so bad now... as once. And it 'elp me to talk to you, you
know.

OSBORNE: All I can do is very little.

JEANNE: Never mind, it do me good. I 'ope to see you some other time?

OSBORNE: I'll probably see you fairly often. I'm starting on the country
round next week, and I'll be calling out your way.

JEANNE: Oh, that is fine. I shall look forward to your coming,
monsieur... but I am not very good customer.

OSBORNE: Never mind, we can have a talk about old times, at any rate.

JEANNE: And I will make a cup of tea... like dinkum Aussie!

OSBORNE: Splendid! That's a bargain, now?

JEANNE: A bargain!

> *They laugh and shake hands across the counter. At this moment*
> JIM *comes out of Ritchie's office. His face is strained and a little
> haggard. He pauses a moment, looking at the door he has just
> closed and* JEANNE *runs forward and takes his arm.*

Oh... Jim... come 'ere! 'Ere is someone who 'ave been to Paree.

> *She turns to* OSBORNE, *who has come from behind the counter so
> that he meets* JIM *halfway.*

Monsieur, this is my 'usband. Jim, 'e knows all about Paree and
'ave been there lots of times.

JIM: Well, if it isn't Cliff Osborne! Where on earth did you spring from?

> *Their hands meet in a hearty grip.*

OSBORNE: I just thought I'd look you all up.

JEANNE: You are friends? You know each other?

OSBORNE: Jim and I went off to enlist together. That's a long time ago,
Jim.

JIM: Too right it is.

JEANNE: [*turning to* MISS PATTERSON] Is it not strange? 'Ere I 'ave
been talking to monsieur like 'e was old friend, and now I find 'e
is old friend.

MISS PATTERSON: There's no–one in this town who did not know Mr Osborne, Mrs Davidson.

OSBORNE: I was the town's bad boy, not like old Jim here, who was always the shining example.

JIM: [*with a shade of irritation*] Shining example of a grafter, you mean. It's all very well for fellows like you with no responsibilities. You're the ones that can get a kick out of life.

OSBORNE: [*jokingly*] And what have I got out of life compared with you? Here you are, a prosperous young farmer, happily married... the backbone of the country!

JIM: Not too much of the prosperous!

> *Suddenly* JEANNE *realises* JIM's *mission with Ritchie. All her gaiety dies and she lays a hand on his arm.*

JEANNE: Oh, Jim... what did 'e say?

JIM: Who?

JEANNE: Ritchie.

JIM: Oh, never mind about that now.

JEANNE: But tell me, Jim... what was it... Yes or No?

JIM: [*with difficulty*] No!

CURTAIN

ACT TWO

SCENE ONE

JEANNE's *kitchen.*

Three months have passed and the summer is at its height. The sweltering heat is beating through the iron roof into the hessian–lined kitchen in the two–roomed hut that serves JIM *and* JEANNE *for home. The flat ugliness has been a little lessened by the gay print curtains that* JEANNE *has hung about the windows and the mantelpiece above the stove. Coloured supplements from periodicals have been pasted on to the hessian walls and a further attempt at brightness has been made by growing slips of red geranium in empty jam tins and setting them along the ledge of the two windows at the back. Some chintz cushions and two cane arm–chairs are the sole hints of comfort. In the wall at the back, between the two windows, is a door, and when this is opened the white blaze of the sunlight streams in from the plains outside. The room is slightly dimmed by reason of the hessian blinds that* JIM *has hung outside the two open windows, but the relief they afford is somewhat lessened by the fact that they flap with maddening monotony in the north wind that howls outside. The room is furnished with a meat–safe, a dresser, a couple of windsor chairs, a table, set well forward, a second table, so narrow as to be almost a bench, standing under the window at right, and a kerosene tin standing on the floor beside it, doing duty as a water bucket. Behind the door is an up–ended petrol case. On this stands a water jug and wash–hand basin. On a peg above it hangs a towel. On the stove, which is in the right–hand wall, is a kettle and a saucepan, both blackened with use and age. On the shelf above it is a row of canisters and an old–fashioned clock. In the opposite wall is a door which gives access to the only other room in the house. When the curtain rises* MRS DAVIDSON *is seated by the table near the front, reading a local paper.* JEANNE *is sweeping up some dust off the floor. She uses a small hearth–brush and a dustpan. She is dressed in a simple frock of cotton print, but even this becomes her and she has graced it with neat white cuffs and collar. She pauses near the door, opens it and looks through.*

JEANNE: Name of heaven… what a country!

> *She speaks softly, as though to herself, shuts the door again and resumes her work.* MRS DAVIDSON *looks up sourly but does not reply.*

MRS DAVIDSON: I see where fat lambs are fetching thirty–two shillings.

JEANNE: [*indifferently*] Yes?

MRS DAVIDSON: Wherever did fat lambs come from, I'd like to know? It's a marvel to me how someone always seems to make good out of other people's misfortunes. Here's us without a lamb that's fit to sell and others are getting thirty–two shillings for fats.

> JEANNE *opens the front of the stove, empties in the dust and shuts it with a bang.*

JEANNE: Would you like a cup of tea, maman?

MRS DAVIDSON: Well, I could do with one before I go, and I don't suppose Jim'll be much longer now.

JEANNE: No, I don't suppose so.

MRS DAVIDSON: [*fanning herself with the paper*] Poor boy, what a day to have to go into town. These days that he has to go in and see Ritchie are terrible for him. This last three months since he started to turn nasty have played up with Jim something cruel. I hope to goodness he has some good news this time.

JEANNE: [*making tea at the stove*] I pray to God 'e 'ave!

MRS DAVIDSON: If you pray to old Nick you're more likely to get a word in with Ritchie. I'm sure I don't know why he's so hard on Jim. It seems to me he's worse on Jim than he is to anybody else. Oh, I don't know why he wanted to go and buy this other place, we'd never a' been in this fix if it wasn't for that.

JEANNE: Jim is going to get through all right…

MRS DAVIDSON: I don't see how you can say that. In a few weeks time we'll have to hand–feed the sheep, and where's the money coming from for that?

JEANNE: Oh, never mind about that. This rain will come… it must come… if only this wind would drop!

As she says this there is loathing in her voice.

MRS DAVIDSON: That wind won't stop until it's blown what grass we
 have got into someone else's paddock. I know it!

JEANNE: It is a devil. O God!... 'Ow I 'ate that wind!

MRS DAVIDSON: Well, it's no use swearing at it. Swearing never did no
 good to anything.

JEANNE: [*fighting for calm*] Shall I pour... tea?

MRS DAVIDSON: Leave it there and let it cool.

 Silence while JEANNE *pours out two cups of tea.*

I'd put some of that up in a jug, if I was you. Jim'll be glad of it
when he gets home.

 JEANNE *does not reply, but she goes across to the dresser, takes
 down a jug, fills it with tea, returns to the dresser, opens a
 drawer, takes out a net 'fly dodger', and hangs it over the mouth
 of the jug, the bead fringe tinkling sharply in the silence.* MRS
 DAVIDSON *is still reading her paper and, as* JEANNE *is busy with
 the tea, she bends down and slips off her shoes. She does not
 take her eyes off the paper and wriggles her toes as though they
 have been cramped and hot. She looks up and takes a sip of tea
 as* JEANNE *seats herself at the other end of the table.*

It must be terrible at the saleyards today.

JEANNE: I am not thinking of the saleyards today.

MRS DAVIDSON: Then how'd you like to be Jim and have to stand there?
 Goodness knows what time they'll sell the horses. Did he have any
 trouble getting Colette to lead?

JEANNE: No... she went quite easily. She did not know she was never
 coming back.

MRS DAVIDSON: Well, of course she didn't. What did you expect? You
 always treated that horse as if she was a human being.

JEANNE: Well, what does it matter if I did? I love 'er and she thought
 that I was... wonderful!

MRS DAVIDSON: It's to be hoped that Jim gets a decent price for her,
 anyhow, though I very much doubt if he will. You should have sold
 her months ago when you had a good offer from the doctor, instead
 of keeping her here, eating her head off and costing Jim a small

fortune for feed.

JEANNE: Yes... I know... I know... I 'ave been told all that before.

She jumps to her feet and seizes one of the flapping blinds in an effort to fasten it down.

MRS DAVIDSON: What's the matter with you now?

JEANNE: This blind! They drive me mad!

MRS DAVIDSON: Something's always driving you mad. You want something to think about if you let a little thing like that get on your mind.

JEANNE: Something to think about! Do you think I 'ave nothing to think about?

MRS DAVIDSON: [*setting down her paper majestically*] That's enough from you, young woman. I won't stand for none of your nasty foreign temper, so don't you think I will.

JEANNE: [*seating herself again*] Oh... I am sorry... but you cannot understand. If you only knew the terrible anxiety... and Jim so sick... and 'is 'ead...

MRS DAVIDSON: His head? What did Dr Wilson say about it?

JEANNE: Jim 'as not seen 'im yet.

MRS DAVIDSON: I thought he was going to last time he went in.

JEANNE: Dr Wilson was not there. 'E 'ad been called away.

MRS DAVIDSON: Then is he going to see him today?

JEANNE: Yes, today.

MRS DAVIDSON: Well, if he doesn't, I'll have to talk to him about it myself. I never heard of such a lot of nonsense as Jim's refusing to go when he's as bad as he makes out he is. 'Tisn't as though expense matters either, as we're on the lodge. I'll have it out with him proper if he hasn't been when he gets home to–night.

JEANNE: Oh, no, I wouldn't do that... I wouldn't really.

MRS DAVIDSON: Why not? You're as bad as he is the way you go on. Anybody'd think Jim had something the matter that he didn't want the doctor to tell him about.

JEANNE: That's just it.

MRS DAVIDSON: Did I ever hear the like? What's Jim got to be frightened of after all this time? He's going on like a baby and I'll give him a good sound talking to when he gets home.

JEANNE: [*patiently*] Oh, no, don't do that. That won't do Jim any good. I know 'ow 'e feels. 'E just can't bring 'imself to tell the doctor that the old pain 'as come back... and the fear...

MRS DAVIDSON: But... heavens alive!... Dr Wilson isn't going to shut him in a madhouse.

JEANNE: [*springing to her feet*] Oh... don't say things like that! 'Ow can you... after... after...

MRS DAVIDSON: There you go again. No wonder Jim's nothing but a bundle of nerves. What he wants is some good sound common sense, instead of all this head–stroking I've seen you at by the hour.

JEANNE: Oh... please... please let us alone! You 'ave not been with Jim through all that time like I 'ave and you can never understand what is best for 'im when 'e is bad.

MRS DAVIDSON: Not understand! Isn't Jim my own son? I guess I knew a little about him before you did...

> She draws her breath for further elaboration of the subject, but, before she can do so, there is a knock at the door. Glad of the interruption JEANNE opens it and finds HARRY, the butcher boy, grinning cheerfully at her.

JEANNE: Oh... it is you, 'Arry!

HARRY: Afternoon, Mis' Davidson!

MRS DAVIDSON: Well, Harry?

HARRY: [*to* JEANNE] I couldn't get you any steak, Mis' Davidson, so I had to bring you a bit of mutton.

JEANNE: Mutton? Oh... 'Arry!

HARRY: Don't you like mutton, Mis' Davidson?

JEANNE; I 'ate the very sight of it! I 'ope I never 'ave to eat of it again.

HARRY: [*scratching his head*] Well... I tell you what, I've got a bit of tripe here. How'll that do? It was ordered for Mis' Ryan, but I'll give her the mutton if you like.

JEANNE: Tripe? On a day like this! It is marvellous 'ow you men can eat at all. Well, give it to me, it is better than mutton.

HARRY: Right–oh!

> He departs to get the tripe.

MRS DAVIDSON: I don't know what you want to go buying meat for at all at the price it is when Jim is killing every day.

JEANNE: Well, I cannot 'elp it, it makes me sick to even think of it. Is it not enough that the poor sheep must starve to death without we must eat them when they die?

MRS DAVIDSON: I don't suppose it makes much difference to the sheep what happens to it, as long as it is dead.

> HARRY *comes back to the door and hands* JEANNE *a moist parcel.*

Harry, you'll be passing the post office, won't you?

HARRY: Yes, Mis' Davidson.

MRS DAVIDSON: Then I'll get you to post a letter for me. I meant to give it to Jim and forgot.

> *She stoops down, pulls on her shoes and crosses to the door leading to the other room.* JEANNE *puts the tripe into a dish of water. It stands on the table under the window and she dips water out of the kerosene bucket on the floor.*

HARRY: I say, Mis' Davidson, did you know the fence in the fifty–acre paddock was down?

JEANNE: The fence in the fifty–acre paddock? Is it, 'Arry?

HARRY: I don't think it has been down long. The sheep had just started to get through when I came along. I fixed it up a bit and I think it'll keep them out for a while, but you want to tell Jim about it. The big water–hole is there and they'll drown as quick as anything if they get in the mud.

JEANNE: I know. Jim is always afraid of that. It won't be long now till 'e comes. I'll tell him straight away.

MRS DAVIDSON: [*re–entering*] Did you see my bag about, Jan?

JEANNE: You 'ad it 'ere this afternoon. [*Looking around and seeing it on a chair*] 'Ere it is.

MRS DAVIDSON: That's right. Ta. Here's the letter, Harry. Don't forget it, will you?

HARRY: [*sticking it in the band of his hat*] No, Mis' Davidson.

MRS DAVIDSON: [*sitting down again*] That's a good boy.

JEANNE: Would you like a cup of tea, 'Arry?

HARRY: I think I'll just take a drink out of your water–bag, if you don't mind, Mis' Davidson.

JEANNE: That's right, 'Arry. Take it as you pass. It is under the tree out there, though I don't suppose it will be very cool on a day like this.

HARRY: Find it hot enough today, Mis' Davidson?

JEANNE: 'Ot enough? 'Oly mother!… 'Ot enough!

Her vehemence amuses him and he grins up at her.

HARRY: Tell you what, I'll be passing the coolstores on my way back. I'll fetch you a bit of ice if you like.

JEANNE: Oh, 'Arry, I should love it!

HARRY: Right–oh! When I've finished up this round then. [*Taking a pencil from behind his ear and a book from his pocket*] Any order for Friday, Mis' Davidson?

JEANNE: [*with a look at her mother–in–law*] No… nothing, thank you, 'Arry.

HARRY: Oh! Good–oh! So long, Mis' Davidson.

With a smile that includes them both, he touches his hat and disappears from the doorway.

JEANNE: Nice boy, 'Arry.

MRS DAVIDSON: [*reading the paper again*] Yes, Harry's the best of that lot.

JEANNE: Another cup of tea, maman?

MRS DAVIDSON: No, I've still got some. I see Cliff Osborne has been put on the committee of the tennis club. Funny how everybody makes such a fuss of a fellow like that. He's running the dance to–night, too.

JEANNE: [*walking across to look out the door*] Yes, I 'eard that. Is Nelly going?

MRS DAVIDSON: Yes, she's going. She stayed at home today to get her dress fixed.

JEANNE: Fancy dress?

MRS DAVIDSON: No, not Nelly! If others like to make a guy of themselves, you won't catch her doing it.

JEANNE: Well, she knows best.

JEANNE is talking automatically, her eyes are fixed on a point far beyond the open door.

MRS DAVIDSON: [*reading aloud*] Here you are. 'The dance that has been organised by Mr Clifford Osborne is to take place in the Mechanics' Hall to–night and promises to be one of the most successful functions of the year. Many novelties have been planned, amongst which is the grand parade of fancy costumes and a waltzing competition.' Grand parade and waltzing competition! We're getting quite lively!

JEANNE: 'Ere is Jim coming now!

The old woman jumps up, goes to the door and almost elbows JEANNE *out of the way.*

MRS DAVIDSON: Yes, that's him. Well, thank goodness we'll soon know.

JEANNE: 'E 'asn't got 'er.

MRS DAVIDSON: Hasn't got her? What on earth are you talking about?

JEANNE: Colette 'as gone!

MRS DAVIDSON: [*hand on hips*] Well, my lands! Is that all you can think of at a time like this? A bit of a horse when you might be turned out of house and home for all you know.

JEANNE: Oh, why is it that no matter what I say, it is the wrong thing? I worry about Jim, but I 'ave loved Colette... Surely I can feel a little sad?

MRS DAVIDSON: There's time enough to think of that when we know the rest. Jim'll soon get another horse if things go all right.

JEANNE: I'll never 'ave another 'orse!

MRS DAVIDSON: There you are. Who's being contrary now?

JEANNE: [*under her breath*] O God!

She turns away from the doorway so that the mother is there alone when JIM *comes in. He is tired and dejected and hardly looks up at her greeting.*

MRS DAVIDSON: Well, son?

JEANNE *comes forward, her eyes fixed on his face. They are wide with fear, already she seems to read disaster.*

Well?

JIM: [*flinging down his hat and slumping into a chair*] No luck!

There is a silence.

MRS DAVIDSON: No luck?

JEANNE *does not speak or move, only her expressive mouth trembles a little.*

JIM: No. Any tea, Jeanne?

JEANNE *comes to herself and hastens across to take the jug of tea from the dresser and give it to him.*

MRS DAVIDSON: What happened, Jim? What does it mean?

JIM: Seven days to pay... or get out!

MRS DAVIDSON: Seven days!

She flops into a chair and bursts into loud weeping

Oh... I knew it would come to this... I knew it would.

JIM: Oh, shut up, ma! What the hell's the good of going on like that?

MRS DAVIDSON: Why shouldn't I go on like this? Isn't it my home that's going to be sold up? I should never a' signed it over to you the way I did. Oh, what am I going to do? What am I going to do?

JIM: Will you stop that row? God damn it all, haven't I had enough to stand today without having you go on like that?

JEANNE: Jim... Jim... don't speak like that. [*Going to the mother's side*] Dear... please don't cry... please. Listen, we 'ave got a week, that is something. We only need the rain to come before then and we can get some money on our sheep.

MRS DAVIDSON: Rain! We'll get no rain for weeks.

JIM: If I can get fifty pounds together to meet the interest, the old devil can't touch me.

JEANNE: Fifty pounds! Why, surely we can get that much. Jim... that should not be hard.

JIM: It might as well be five hundred. We simply haven't got it.

JEANNE: Then we must get it.

MRS DAVIDSON: To hear her talk you'd think that five–pound notes grew on every bush.

JEANNE: [*valiantly*] Well, think of all the money in the world, surely we can get such a little bit of it.

MRS DAVIDSON: What's all the money in the world got to do with us? We're going to be turned out of house and home for the want of fifty pounds.

JIM: Oh, ma... do dry up!

MRS DAVIDSON: There's a son for you... to speak to me like that when you've ruined me with your big ideas. Going and buying another farm you hadn't the money to pay for.

JIM: [*jumping up*] Oh... for God's sake! [*Controlling himself*] Look, ma, I'm too tired to talk about things like that now. I've been at it all day and I want a rest. Put your things on and let me take you home. I left the horse in on purpose.

MRS DAVIDSON: All right, I suppose I'd best be getting home. But it does seem awful.

JIM: I'm sorry, ma... but you come over tomorrow and we'll talk it over then.

MRS DAVIDSON: All right.

> *She dries her eyes and, sniffling miserably, goes into the other room to get her hat.* JIM *crosses to where the jug and basin stand behind the door and commences to wash his hands.*

JEANNE: Jim... who bought 'er?

JIM: Who?

JEANNE: Colette.

JIM: Oh, Dr Wilson.

JEANNE: Dr Wilson! Oh, I am so glad. 'E will be kind to 'er. 'Ow much did she fetch, Jim?

JIM: Six pounds.

JEANNE: Six pounds! Only six pounds?

JIM: Well, I don't think that's too bad, considering...

JEANNE: I think it is terrible. For the sake of six pounds to have to send 'er away.

JIM: It isn't the money we got for her, it's the price of feed, and we couldn't let her starve.

JEANNE: No... that's right. My poor little pet, she won't have to go searching round 'er box for the last little bit of chaff now. She used to stand at the gate out there and call to me every time I went past; it was terrible to 'ave no food to give 'er.

> JIM *dries his hands, hangs the towel back on the nail and puts a comforting arm about her.*

JIM: Cheer up, old girl... we'll buy her back one of these days.

JEANNE: Will we, Jim?

JIM: You bet your life we will. She'll be quite happy where she is and you know that Dr Wilson will look after her as well as you did.

JEANNE: Yes, I suppose so, but she will miss me, Jim.

JIM: [*matter–of–factly*] Oh... she might, for a few days. Well, here's your money, anyhow. You save it up and we'll get her back when things are better.

> JEANNE *takes it without a word.* MRS DAVIDSON *comes in again. She is wearing the hat with the disputed pink roses well to the fore. She is hot and perspiring.*

MRS DAVIDSON: My stars, that room of yours is like an oven. It beats me how you two can get a wink of sleep.

JIM: [*picking up his hat*] Sleep! I haven't slept for nights.

MRS DAVIDSON: Then why don't you come back with me? You can have your old room and it's as cool as a cucumber there.

> JEANNE *says nothing but her eyes travel from one face to another.*

JIM: No thanks, ma. We're quite comfortable here. It's not the heat that keeps me awake. Are you ready now?

MRS DAVIDSON: Yes, I'm ready. But I don't see why you'd rather stick in a little shanty like this instead of living in the big house that was your father's before you and where you ought to be.

JIM: Now, ma. We've had all that out before. We tried living with you and you know it didn't work.

MRS DAVIDSON: And whose fault was that, I'd like to know? You're the only son I've got and it isn't right that you should go as far away as you can and let me and Nelly live there alone.

JIM: [*calmly and decisively*] And it isn't right that Jeanne shouldn't have a home of her own, either. We're only a mile away from you, ma, so you're not so very much alone.

MRS DAVIDSON: You're only a mile away because you can't get no further!

JIM: Now look, ma, it's no use you going on like that; Jeanne and I are getting on fine and we like it here, even though it isn't very grand.

MRS DAVIDSON: Oh, very well, if she prefers to stop here in a little two–roomed hut to living in a decent house with me... that's all there is to be said about it.

JEANNE: That's not right!

JIM: Now Jeanne... be quiet!

JEANNE: Jim, I will not be quiet. I 'ave listened to things like that from 'er all the afternoon and I 'ave 'ad enough. This is my 'ouse and I don't care if it is a little two–roomed hut... I will not 'ave it called so... like she does!

MRS DAVIDSON: She! I like the way you speak about me!

JEANNE: You 'ate me... I know it, and why don't you say so, instead of coming 'ere, pretending to be friendly, and trying to get Jim away from me and from this place... the only thing that I 'ave got to call my own.

JIM: Look here, cut it out, you two. I've just about had enough for one day without any more of this sort of thing. If you two can't get together without fighting, you'd better keep apart. Are you coming, ma?

JEANNE: Oh... Jim!

MRS DAVIDSON: Yes, I'm coming. I've had just about enough for one day, too.

She stalks out without a glance in JEANNE's *direction.*

JIM: [*contritely*] I'll be back soon.

He follows his mother, leaving JEANNE *standing alone. For a second or two she looks after them with clenched hands and set teeth; she gives a little stifled cry of futile temper, then turns and commences to clear some of the cups, etc. off the table. She seats herself by the table and takes the little roll of notes from the front of her dress and lays them out before her one by one.*

JEANNE: One... two... three... four... five... six. Not enough for anything!

She sighs deeply and looks straight ahead, so that she does not notice OSBORNE *as he steps into the doorway.*

OSBORNE: Hello there!

JEANNE: Why, monsieur Osborne!

She gathers up the money and springs to greet him.

Oh, 'ow nice to see you!

OSBORNE: [*coining inside and setting down a bag*] I was passing this way and couldn't resist the temptation of dropping in.

He takes off his hat, wipes around the band with his handkerchief, and dries his perspiring face.

JEANNE: No. That is fine. Sit down. Would you like a cup of tea? See, it is all ready to make.

OSBORNE: No, don't you trouble about me. I had a drink a little while ago.

JEANNE: But let me give you a cup of tea?

OSBORNE: No, really... I'd rather not.

JEANNE: Very well, then.

She crosses to where he is standing near the table.

OSBORNE: Cigarette?

JEANNE: [*with a glance out of the door*] Merci!

They light up and seat themselves, one at either end of the table.

OSBORNE: Well... how's things?

JEANNE's answer is a gesture which is rich with eloquence.

Like that, is it?

JEANNE: It is terrible, monsieur. More terrible than I ever could 'ave thought.

OSBORNE: Jim's sheep still dying?

JEANNE: [*with a slow nod*] Every day I think that there will surely be no more die tomorrow, but every morning, when I get up and look out of that door there, I see them lying on the ground, too weak to get up, and the crows... Oh, why did God ever make such awful things as those crows?

OSBORNE: I know.

A little silence while they both smoke.

JEANNE: [*looking out of the open door*] It seems 'ard to believe that there was ever grass on those plains out there. Not a blade... not a leaf!

OSBORNE: And yet, when the rain comes, it won't be a week before you see them turning green again and, within a month, all your sheep will be fat.

JEANNE: The rain! Is it ever going to come in time? Oh, monsieur, when I 'ave shivered in the snow and sleet of Paree, I never thought that I would come to curse that sunshine as I 'ave done.

OSBORNE: Sunny Australia, eh?

JEANNE: [*intensely*] 'Ow long would you say that it will be before it comes?

OSBORNE: The rain? That's hard to say. You can't judge these things.

JEANNE: Sometimes I feel that it is not going to come until everything is lost… everything is ruined… and then, when it is too late, God will laugh at me… and send his rain.

OSBORNE: Now that's a cheerful little thought! How did you come to drop on that?

JEANNE: Because, one by one, all the things that I 'ad 'oped for 'ave been taken from me. Why not this? Oh… I 'ave not been very lucky for the Davidsons. I sometimes think that Jim made a big mistake.

OSBORNE: Who's been putting that into your head?

JEANNE: No–one's been putting that into my 'ead. I know it. Don't you think yourself it would 'ave been ever so much better if Jim and I 'ad never met one another?

OSBORNE: That's a lot of damned rot, and you know it. Has Jim ever hinted such a thing?

JEANNE: Not Jim… never.

OSBORNE: Who has then? His mother?

> JEANNE *nods dumbly.*

You're surely not such a silly little goose as to let that spiteful old devil come between you and Jim? That's all she's after. Don't let her pull it off.

JEANNE: Oh… it's not only 'er.

OSBORNE: Who else has been bothering you?

JEANNE: [*fiercely*] Why does no–one like me? Why does no–one treat me like a decent woman? Everybody seems to think because I come from Paree that I am a little… odd… not quite right… not the kind of woman they would like to make a friend of.

OSBORNE: Oh… rubbish!

JEANNE: It is not rubbish. I make mistakes when I first come out, I know I do. I take the 'and of some… I smile at some I do not know, but what is that? It is not enough to make them treat me as they do.

OSBORNE: And how do they treat you?

JEANNE: Like as if I 'ad been… bad.

OSBORNE: Oh… go… on! What on earth makes you say that?

JEANNE: The way they look at me… speak to me.

OSBORNE: Jeanne… don't be silly. You're imagining all this.

JEANNE: Imagining it? Not I! Sometimes, monsieur, I get so lonely, I wish that I might die. There is not a soul but you to talk to me of 'ome... not one who try to get to know... or who care.

OSBORNE: [*less casually than before*] Look here, you've got the wrong idea of things altogether. Australians are the friendliest people under the sun, you've just got them all wrong.

JEANNE: [*getting up to stub her cigarette on the stove*] And they've got me all wrong. So there it is. Oh well, it can't be 'elped. We are two different kinds of people and nothing is going to alter that, is it? Now, show me all the pretty things that you 'ave got in that bag of yours, and we'll forget all about it.

She is once again her old, gay self, and advances to the table.

OSBORNE: But I don't like to hear you talk like that.

JEANNE: [*smiling*] And you won't 'ear it any more, so there! What 'ave you got this time?

OSBORNE *gets up and lifts the bag on to the table.*

OSBORNE: Here you are. Open it up yourself.

JEANNE *opens the bag and spreads out the contents. It is full of light and airy materials.*

JEANNE: Oh, 'ow pretty! Are they not pretty?

OSBORNE: I thought you'd like them.

JEANNE: Monsieur, you are a dear, the way you bring these things for me to see.

OSBORNE: Why shouldn't I? Business is business, you know, and some day I'll make a sale.

JEANNE: Business! That is what you call your good 'eart, monsieur. [*Turning again to the materials*] Oh, look at that! Isn't it pretty?

She has found a length of satin. She picks it up and it catches unpleasantly on the rough skin on her hands.

Ugh!

OSBORNE: What's the matter?

JEANNE: Look.

OSBORNE: [*taking the hand she holds out*] What have you been doing to your hands?

JEANNE: What 'ave I been doing? This stove, these pots and pans... is it any wonder they are like they are?

OSBORNE: There's nothing the matter with them.

JEANNE: [*withdrawing her hand*] That is nice of you, monsieur, but the satin tell me different.

OSBORNE: Then the satin doesn't know what it's talking about, so don't take any notice of it. Have a look at something else. How about this?

JEANNE: Yes, it is nice, but not so nice as satin. There is nothing so lovely to a woman as silk. It feels so nice.

OSBORNE: If it's silk you want, have a look in the bottom of the bag.

JEANNE: Something in the bottom of the bag?

> *She commences to rummage through it*

What a pretty piece of lace. Is that it, monsieur?

OSBORNE: No, not that.

JEANNE: This?

OSBORNE: No, it's something special this time. Something you've never seen before.

JEANNE: Oh, you make me quite excited, monsieur. [*Taking out a cardboard box*] Is it in 'ere?

OSBORNE: Yes, that's it.

JEANNE: [*lifting the lid*] It is something pink!

OSBORNE: You bet your life it is!

JEANNE: [*with the box open*] Why, monsieur!… Oh… 'ow beautiful! Oh, the darling, darling little things.

> *Her voice drops to a lovely minor key and, one by one, she lifts out the contents of the box, the dainty, filmy loveliness of a set of silk lingerie. She lifts them to her face and her voice is full of tears as she speaks.*

Oh, the touch of silk against my skin. 'Ow often have I thought of it. You do not know what it reminds me of. Paree… perfume and powder… 'appiness… all the lovely things that I 'ave lost… forever.

> *Her voice breaks so that she cannot go on.* OSBORNE *watches her in silence. The moment is too poignant for words.*

They make me cry, monsieur. [*Touching each one with wistful fingers*] They are beautiful!

OSBORNE: I knew you'd like them. As soon as I saw them I thought they seemed to belong to you.

JEANNE: So did I!

OSBORNE: Are you going to have them?

JEANNE: 'Ave them? You mean, buy them?

OSBORNE: Why not?

JEANNE: Don't be foolish. What use 'ave I for things like these?

OSBORNE: Use! Jeanne, I'm surprised at you. Things like that aren't meant to be useful, they're far too beautiful.

JEANNE: Maybe, but I'm a poor man's wife.

OSBORNE: Therefore far more in need of pretty things than a rich man's wife.

JEANNE: [*commencing to fold them away*] Now, monsieur, you must not tempt me like that.

OSBORNE: Far be it from me to tempt you, but I'd like to see you have them. There's really not another woman in the district who would appreciate them like you would.

JEANNE: Then they'll 'ave to go to someone who 'as plenty of money and no imagination... poor darlings!

OSBORNE: It's paying for them that's the trouble, is it?

JEANNE: Why, of course!

OSBORNE: Well, you needn't pay for them all at once, you know.

JEANNE: Oh, no... bit by bit, and then, when they are all worn out, I am still paying for them.

OSBORNE: But if they give you any pleasure...

JEANNE: They certainly do that.

OSBORNE: Well, you get little enough of it... why not take what you can?

JEANNE *is sorely tempted and touches the pretty things longingly.*

JEANNE: 'Ow much did you say they cost, monsieur?

OSBORNE: Only six pounds for the lot.

JEANNE: Six pounds!

OSBORNE: That's all.

JEANNE: [*bitterly*] It isn't very much, is it?

OSBORNE: Not when it's for something that you like very much.

JEANNE: Not when it's for something that you love very much!

She is thinking of Colette. After a moment of indecision she draws a deep breath and turns impulsively to OSBORNE.

Monsieur, I think you are right. I need these things... to make up for other things.

OSBORNE: Splendid! I told you I'd be booking an order some day.

JEANNE: Not book. I will pay you now. I 'ave got the money 'ere.

OSBORNE: Just as you like, of course.

JEANNE *takes the money from the front of her dress and puts it on the table.*

JEANNE: Six pounds! All the money I possess... and I buy a set of silk lingerie! There are plenty of people in this world, monsieur, who would blame me for doing that, but they 'ave never known what it is like to be almost at the end of... everything, nor 'ow much a little bit of pleasure can 'elp at such a time and place... as this.

OSBORNE: [*taking up the money and writing in a book*] If they give you any help...

JEANNE: They do. And I feel I need 'elp... terribly.

OSBORNE: [*casually*] Then you're quite right in getting it whatever way you can. [*Putting down his book and starting to fold the lingerie*] I'm afraid I'll have to take this lot away with me this afternoon; they're a sample line, but I'll see that you get your order tomorrow, without fail.

JEANNE: That will be all right, monsieur. I will 'ave them soon enough.

OSBORNE: It's a pity you couldn't have them now, they'd be just the thing for the dance to–night.

JEANNE: [*laughing*] Oh, I don't think that there will be much dance for me to–night.

OSBORNE: Why not? I thought you said you were coming along.

JEANNE: I don't think I will be able to.

OSBORNE: Won't Jim go?

JEANNE: Jim never did care much for dancing.

OSBORNE: But what about you?

JEANNE: I? Oh, I 'ave not danced for years.

OSBORNE: Now that's a jolly shame. Listen to me, you and Jim are just the ones who should go out. Get away from things for a while. No one can stand too much of this sort of thing without a break. If you won't speak to Jim, I'll jolly well do it myself.

JEANNE: Oh, monsieur, what is the use? Look... I show you something. Do you see that knife up there? Every day that knife is taken down to kill sheep, the sheep that are our living and, every night it is so blunt, Jim have to take a stone and sharpen it... so that it will be ready to begin again tomorrow. Do you think that I could ask 'im to take me out to dance?

OSBORNE: But don't you think that the things you want to do are just as important as things he doesn't want to do?

JEANNE: Monsieur, it is kind of you to bother about me.

OSBORNE: Kind be hanged!

He has been packing up his wares as he talks and puts the last of them into the suitcase. He closes it with a snap and turns towards her.

Don't think I'm trying to interfere by persuading you to come to this dance. It's none of my business, I know, but I feel that you've got a grievance, and a good one. You've had a rotten spin out here, you've met up with all the wrong people and I want the chance to show you some of the others. There'll be some jolly nice folks at this dance and you'll like them, that's why I want you to come along.

JEANNE: Monsieur, I'll come if I can. But, you understand 'ow things are, don't you?

OSBORNE: Jeanne, I understand a whole lot. I know what it's like to be at breaking point. I've been there myself.

He is ready to go. Suddenly he takes a step forward and takes her hand.

Jeanne... if there's ever anything that I can do to make things easier for you... you know you've only got to say the word, don't you?

JEANNE: Yes, I know.

OSBORNE: That's all right then.

He puts on his hat, squares his shoulders and prepares to go, a little ashamed of the emotion he has displayed.

Till to–night, then.

JEANNE: Till to–night, perhaps.

They smile and shake hands with one another in the good fellowship that comes with complete understanding. JIM *comes to the open door. He pauses at the sight of them, then steps inside.*

OSBORNE: Hello there, Jim. Haven't seen you for ages.

JIM: No, I haven't been in lately.

OSBORNE: How's things?

JIM: [*flinging down his hat*] Not too wonderful. How're they with you?

OSBORNE: Not too bad. Had a nice win on Saturday. Picked a double at fifty–to–one.

JIM *looks at his cheerful, smiling face.* OSBORNE *is everything that* JIM *is not: carefree, happy, affluent.*

JIM: You would!

He turns away.

OSBORNE: Oh well, I'll be getting along. So long, Mrs Davidson… so long, Jim.

JIM & JEANNE: [*together*] Good–bye.

After he has gone there is a little silence as JIM *takes off his coat and hangs it behind the door. He rolls up the sleeves of his shirt and loosens his collar.*

JIM: [*irritably*] What's that fellow been doing here all this time?

JEANNE: 'E 'as not been 'ere so very long.

JIM: [*sarcastically*] Well, it's been more than five minutes since I passed him coming in the side gate.

JEANNE: And it's not two hours ago, either!

She has been trying to fasten down the blind and turns away from it, defeated by the wind.

JIM: You've been crying. What have you been talking about?

JEANNE: I do not remember what we 'ave been talking about. Monsieur Osborne 'ave some things to show me. What do you think we talk about?

JIM*'s manner has annoyed her and she moves impatiently about the kitchen, busy at small things.* JIM *seats himself at the table, his eyes never off her face.*

JIM: You didn't buy anything, I hope?

JEANNE: No, I didn't buy anything.

JIM: Then what the devil brought him out here?

JEANNE: 'Ow should I know?

JIM: There's not a week goes by but he comes hanging round. You must tell him to come.

JEANNE: I do not tell 'im to come!

She turns to face him, on the defensive.

JIM: Then tell him not to come. It's no use him wasting his time here. We owe enough money to Ritchie now without him trying to make it more.

JEANNE: 'E does not try to make it any more. 'E simply come in as he pass and if 'e 'ave any little thing 'e think I like to see, 'e show it to me... and that is all.

JIM: And that's what happened today?

JEANNE: Yes.

JIM: Then what have you been crying about? Been telling him how badly you've been treated?

JEANNE: [*angrily*] Jim... what is the matter with you?

JIM: And what's the matter with you?

JEANNE: What do you mean?

JIM: You know darned well what I mean. Don't think I'm such a blasted fool as I look. I won't have this fellow hanging round here. Do you get that?

JEANNE: Yes... I get that. And I get the reason why you are going on like this, and if that old devil can't mind 'er own business...

JIM: Just leave my mother out of this. She's got nothing to do with it. This is between you and me.

JEANNE: This is between you and me, but it was she who started it. I know. She saw Monsieur Osborne coming 'ere and she talk of it all the way 'ome. I know 'er!

JIM: Well, it's time someone had something to say. So cut him out... see? Tell him he's not wanted.

JEANNE: I will not!

JIM: Oh, won't you?

JEANNE: No, I will not. If there's any telling of that sort to be done, you can do it yourself.

JIM: Then by God, I will, and pretty smart too. Who the hell wants him to come butting in here, anyhow?

JEANNE: I do. He's the only one in this miserable place who still knows 'ow to laugh! I stick out 'ere day after day, with nothing but dust and drought and 'eat and flies, until I think that I will go mad. Do you wonder that I am please to see someone who 'ave got a cheery word and who can make me laugh?

JIM: Then have him! Have him! Go on, clear out with your wonderful Osborne, if you think so much of him!

> *For a moment* JEANNE*'s face is distorted with passion, then she sees how things are with* JIM *and her anger dies. He is shaking from head to foot and his face is twisted with the agony of his twitching nerves. He picks up the jug that stands beside him and tries to pour out some of the cold tea. It spills helplessly on to the table and he drops his head on his arm, shaken by sobs.*

JEANNE: Jim… Jim, you never meant that?

> *She crosses over to the table and stands by his side*

You know, Jim, you and I should never say things like that to one another, should we?

> JIM *cannot reply, but one hand gropes out for hers. She seats herself on the table and raises his head by placing a hand under his chin and turning his face up to hers.*

I never meant the things in the way they sounded, Jim. It is only that I sometimes get a little lonely, and it does me good to talk to someone. You know there's nothing else, don't you, Jim?

> JIM *nods dumbly and drops his head in her lap. She smiles tenderly and wistfully and runs soft fingers through his hair. Slowly his violent trembling ceases and he gains control of himself.*

You know, whatever 'appens… *whatever* 'appens, you and I are going to stand together, Jim. This is an 'ard pull and maybe it is going to be too much for both of us, but it's not going to make any difference between us, is it, Jim?

JIM *shakes his head and puts an arm about her slim waist, clinging desperately to her.*

We need each other, dear, and we need what little 'appiness we can get, you should remember that.

JIM: It isn't Osborne coming here that I mind... and I like to think that you can laugh... still; but it's what might be said about you. Everybody knows that Osborne comes mighty near being a thoroughly bad lot.

JEANNE: But, Jim, don't you know that it's the bad men, and the bad women, who are most likely to do the kindest things and to 'elp you most when you are down? Jim, it's only kindness that 'ave brought Monsieur Osborne 'ere. 'E bring the pretty things that 'e know I love, and if you see that I 'ave cry, it is only because I 'ave seen something that remind me of all the lovely times we 'ad when we were together in Paree... before you got sick, and life got so very hard for us.

This seems to give JIM *pain and he drops his head again into her lap.*

Why, Jim, when I see those things again, I forget all about Monsieur Osborne even being 'ere! When I 'ave all those lovely memories in my 'eart do you think that there would be room for anybody else, silly boy?

JIM: I'm sorry, chérie, but it's partly that that makes me go on the way I do. I know the rotten time you've had, and when I think of those days and all I meant to do for you...

JEANNE: [*placing her hand over his mouth*] Hush!

JIM: [*speaking through her fingers*] I've never said anything about it, Jeanne, because I was afraid I wouldn't be able to pull it off, but I only bought this other place to try and get the things for you that I know you've always wanted.

JEANNE: What do you mean, Jim?

JIM: This other place. I knew I never had a chance with only the old farm; there was only a bare living for us all, so I got ma to let me raise a mortgage and buy the other, so that I could have a shot at clearing up a fortune, and then I was going to take you away for a while, back to Paris and give you some of the pretty things you want.

JEANNE: You did that for me?... Oh, Jim!

JIM: I'm afraid it's a long way off now, dear.

JEANNE: But never mind... never mind... you tried!

JIM: I tried, but that's about all. I'm afraid we're going to be beaten at it.

JEANNE: Oh, we can't be beaten, Jim. Surely we can get that money? Is there no way?

JIM: I don't know. I was thinking about it coming home. I may be able to borrow some from Dave, then ma's got ten pounds she can let me have. We only want fifty pounds to give us three months. I'll have to have that six pounds of yours, Jeanne.

JEANNE: [*with a start of dismay*] My six pounds! What do you mean, Jim?

JIM: The money you got for Colette. I'm sorry to have to ask you for it, kiddie, but it may make all the difference to us.

> JEANNE *is aghast. She opens her mouth to speak, but can find no words.*

With that and the ten pounds ma has and perhaps twenty from Dave, I'll only need fourteen more. It doesn't seem so much then.

JEANNE: [*mechanically*] No... it doesn't, does it?

JIM: [*looking up at her*] You don't mind my asking for it, do you?

JEANNE: No... oh, no... of course not.

> *She gets down from her seat on the table and walks across the room.*

Jim... don't you think Monsieur Osborne would 'elp you too? 'E 'as always been so kind.

JIM: [*with a quick frown*] No... blast Osborne!

JEANNE: But why, Jim? 'E always seem to 'ave plenty of money. Look at what 'e won at the races!

JIM: Well, never mind about him. We'll manage without his help. You let me have what you've got and we'll find a way to get the rest.

JEANNE: [*falteringly*] But, Jim... I 'ave not got it!

JIM: What?

JEANNE: I 'aven't got it!

JIM: But I gave it to you. What have you done with it?

JEANNE: I… bought something.

JIM: You bought something? From Osborne?

JEANNE: Yes.

JIM: You bought something from Osborne! But you just told me you didn't.

JEANNE: I know. I didn't like to tell you when you were so… cross.

JIM: [*his anger beginning to rise*] Do you mean to say you spent your whole six pounds on something that fellow brought out?

JEANNE: It was only such a little bit of money… it was not enough for anything, Jim.

JIM: It might be enough to make all the difference to us. Why, you must be crazy. What on earth made you do such a thing?

JEANNE: [*miserably*] I don't know, Jim.

JIM: Well, what was it? What did you buy?

JEANNE: It was something… for myself.

JIM: Oh, yes… I might have guessed that. What was it?

JEANNE: Oh, you make it all so 'ard! 'Ow can I explain?

JIM: Well, I want to know. God knows we're hard enough up against it without you going and spending practically all the ready cash we own on some darned rubbish we don't need. What was it?

JEANNE: [*stricken with remorse*] It… was… some underclothes!

JIM: Underclothes? What sort of underclothes?

JEANNE: Silk ones.

JIM: Silk underclothes! [*As* JEANNE *nods her head*] Well, I'll be damned!

JEANNE: Oh, Jim, I never thought you'd want the money. I never did!

JIM: You bought a set of silk underclothes from Clifford Osborne! Did he take them out and… *show* them to you?

JEANNE: [*in astonishment*] Yes, Jim.

JIM: He did? Oh! Does he often bring you things like that?

JEANNE: Never before, Jim.

JIM: This is something new, then?

> *He gets up out of his chair and faces her across the narrow little room.*

JEANNE: Oh, Jim, don't be cross with me! I never dreamt that you would want the money. That such a little bit could matter. Truly,

Jim!

JIM: Damn the money! It's not that I'm thinking of, it's that fellow's confounded cheek in selling you a thing like that.

JEANNE: Why, Jim… don't be so absurd! Do you mean those pretty little things I bought?

JIM: Too right I do. What were they?

JEANNE: What were they?

JIM: Yes. What kind of underclothes?

JEANNE: Well… there was a petticoat… and a nightdress…

JIM: Yes? What else?

JEANNE: Oh, Jim… you *do* make it sound a lot!

JIM: Go on!

JEANNE: Well…

She falters before his tremendous disapproval.

JIM: Of course! Well, that certainly finishes it. If I catch that damned fellow here again, I'll kick him from here to blazes!

JEANNE: Jim! Are you mad?

JIM: And you can go into that shop tomorrow and tell them to keep their rotten underclothing and to let you have that money back.

JEANNE: Jim! What are you talking about?

JIM: What the devil do you think I'm talking about? Do you think I'm going to allow you to go on like this? Good God! I never heard the like of it! If you haven't any sense of decency… it's time you were taught a lesson!

JEANNE: Jim! 'Ow dare you!

> HARRY *has come to the door carrying a small sack. He pauses a moment when he discovers that the* DAVIDSONS *are not in a mood to welcome intrusion, then knocks loudly.*

HARRY: Hello, there!

> *Both* JEANNE *and* JIM *turn sharply at the greeting.* JIM *is none too pleased at the interruption.*

JEANNE: 'Ello, 'Arry.

HARRY: Thought I'd call in with that ice I promised.

JEANNE: Oh, that is kind of you, 'Arry. Will you just put it down somewhere?

HARRY *sets the bag down inside the doorway and looks doubtfully across at* JIM.

HARRY: I say, Jim… those sheep of yours have got into that water–hole pretty badly.

JEANNE *gives a gasp of dismay. She has forgotten.*

JIM: What water–hole?

HARRY: Up there in the fifty–acre paddock.

JIM: Fifty–acre paddock? How could they? They'd have to break through the fence.

HARRY *glances at* JEANNE *and there is commiseration in his look.*

JEANNE: Oh, Jim… I forgot to tell you. The fence is down!

JIM: The fence down?

JEANNE: Yes.

JIM: Oh… Christ!

His cry is at once a curse and a prayer.

JEANNE: Oh, 'ow could I forget? 'Ow could I?

JIM: How long have you known?

JEANNE: 'Arry told me. Before you came 'ome.

JIM: Then that's enough! Before your Mister–Bloody–Osborne came!

He strides over to where the butcher's knife is hanging on the wall and reaches up for it.

JEANNE: Jim! What are you going to do?

JIM: What do you think I'll have to do? If the sheep have got to the water–hole, those that haven't got drowned will be smothered in the mud!

JEANNE *gives a little cry of despair and turns away.*

That's right… howl! If you'd been thinking of me instead of chasing after that fellow this wouldn't have happened.

JEANNE *whips around, her eyes blazing at the injustice of his words, but* JIM *takes no notice; he is almost out of the door as he speaks.*

Thanks, Harry.

He pushes past him and disappears.

HARRY: [*awkwardly*] Jolly bad luck… that fence getting down like that.

JEANNE: [*not heeding*] Yes.

HARRY: Well, I guess I'll be getting along, Mis' Davidson. I'm going in to that dance to–night.

JEANNE *turns to look at him, struck by a sudden idea.*

JEANNE: You are going to the dance?

HARRY: Yes. It should be pretty good.

JEANNE: 'Ow are you going in, 'Arry?

HARRY: I got the truck…

JEANNE: 'Ave you? 'Ave you got room for me, 'Arry?

HARRY: Are you going into town to–night, Mis' Davidson?

JEANNE: [*defiantly*] I am going to that dance!

HARRY: Going to the dance? I didn't know.

JEANNE: Well, I am. You wait for me, 'Arry. I won't be long.

She crosses to the bedroom door. HARRY *is thunderstruck.*

HARRY: But what about Jim? What'll he say?

JEANNE: [*her voice quivering with hurt and anger*] 'Arry… Jim cannot say *anything* to me that 'e 'as not said before. For ten years I 'ave done the things that Jim 'as wanted me to do, and now… I'm going to do something that *I* want to do… and I don't care what they say.

She turns and thrusts open the door, leaving the astounded HARRY *gaping after her.*

CURTAIN

SCENE TWO

Eleven o'clock that night.

The curtain rises on JIM *alone in the little kitchen. It is dark and a single oil–lamp gives the only light. He is dressed in shirt and trousers, as in the last scene, his sleeves rolled up and his collar open at the throat. He is seated at the table, gazing straight ahead. He grips a side of the table in either hand, but even this is powerless to stay his violent trembling. Every line and movement reveals intense nervous strain. He gives a start as the clock commences to strike. He watches it until it stops.*

JIM: EIeven!

> *He gets up and lurches to the door. There is nothing beyond but the blackness of the night. He turns into the room again, opens the other door and looks through. He knows he will find no one, but looks because he feels he must look somewhere. He turns back into the middle of the room.*

[*Suddenly and terribly*] Jeanne!… Jeanne! Oh… God Almighty… where are you?

> *He catches his breath in a great sob and flings himself back into the chair. He leans his elbows on the table and grips a side of his head in either hand. He is in the power of a great fear. It will not let him rest. After a few moments he is up again, looking out of the door, then back into the room.*

If only there was somewhere else to look!

> *He moistens his dry lips and turns towards the tin that holds the water. He bends down and dips a cupful out and raises it to his mouth. Suddenly he can hear hurried footsteps in the darkness outside. He sets the cup down and whips around to see who is coming. It is his mother. She comes in hot and breathless, but she, too, is afraid.*

What is it? You've heard something?

MRS DAVIDSON: No, Jim. No one has seen her.

> *She sits heavily in a chair, fanning herself with a handkerchief.*

JIM *stands in the middle of the room.*

I'm sure I don't know what could have come over the girl, clearing off like this without a word to anyone.

JIM: Where have you looked?

MRS DAVIDSON: Everywhere I could think of. I've been this three hours scouring the countryside. To the Smiths, the Thompsons... the Blacks... I'm worn out with it all. And I sent Nelly and Dave in the other direction, to the Williams and the Kents.

JIM: What's the use of going there? Jeanne hardly knows them.

MRS DAVIDSON: You never know what a woman will do when she's in the state Jan is.

JIM: That's just it.

MRS DAVIDSON: Now, Jim, don't you be a fool. Jan's not the one to go and do something silly, no matter what happens.

JIM: Fool! I'm not being a fool, I'm just coming to my senses. We've made her life a hell between the lot of us, do you know that? All the time I've been looking for her to-night I've been remembering... things we've said to her... the poor little kid.

MRS DAVIDSON: Whatever do you mean, Jim?

JIM: She's been ill, and we've expected her to go on working just the same. She's been lonely... homesick... and we've called her discontented. Hell! Do you wonder? When I look at this place... *this* place... and think of what I brought her from, I wonder she stuck it out six months. And just because she still loves pretty things... I said the things to her, that I did say.

MRS DAVIDSON: But still, Jim, even if you did go a bit far, I don't see that there's any great cause to worry. But I do wish she'd come back. She's not got any business stopping out till this hour, goodness knows where.

JIM: If anything happens to Jeanne... I'm through!

MRS DAVIDSON: [*sharply*] Fiddlesticks! Nothing's going to happen to Jan. I know her too well for that.

JIM: What do you know about her? You had her damned from the first minute you got my letter saying I had married a French girl. That was enough for you. No matter what she did, it was the wrong thing in your eyes. All her little mistakes, that anyone else would have smiled at, you talked about and worked on until you made them into crimes… and you made me think the same.

MRS DAVIDSON: I never did nothing of the sort.

JIM: What about this afternoon? What did you have to say about Osborne coming here so often? Doesn't he go to other places as well as this? What did you want to pick on Jeanne for, any more than on Mrs Ryan or Mrs Thompson? Except that no man on earth would look at those old hags!

MRS DAVIDSON: And what do you want to pick on me for? I've said nothing that you haven't thought yourself.

JIM: I didn't think it! I never believed it of Jeanne and nothing on God's earth would ever make me believe wrong of her, but I repeated the rotten things you'd said to me… and now she's gone.

MRS DAVIDSON: I'm sure I don't know why I'm always in the wrong. I've done my best to find her and I'd still be looking if I knew where else to go.

JIM: There's nowhere else we can look. We've got to wait for daylight.

NELLY comes sauntering up to the open doorway. Her face has an expression of malicious triumph.

MRS DAVIDSON: Why, Nelly, you did give me a start! I didn't hear the car come up.

NELLY: Dave's waiting for me at the other gate.

JIM: Have you heard anything, Nelly?

NELLY: [*laughing*] I should say I have.

JIM: You have?

MRS DAVIDSON: What is it, Nell?

NELLY: Something you'd never guess!

JIM: What the devil is it?

NELLY: Your sweet little wife, my dear, has gone to the fancy dress ball! She passed Mrs Ryan, driving on the butcher's cart, at half–past six o'clock this evening.

She gives a mocking little bow in his direction.

MRS DAVIDSON: What? Well, I'll be blessed!

NELLY: Well, now that the panic is over and *my* evening has been thoroughly ruined, I guess I'll be going.

With a last mocking glance at JIM she smiles at her mother and goes.

MRS DAVIDSON: [*laughing shrilly*] Well! If that doesn't beat it all! Gone to the dance! A pretty lot of fools we're going to look when it gets about that we've been running round the district like a lot of scalded cats, scared out of our lives that something had happened to her. As if that young woman'd care what we said to her, as long as she had someone else to tell her different.

JIM: Stop it!

MRS DAVIDSON: What?

JIM: Be quiet, do you hear?

She pauses, but her moment cannot be lost.

MRS DAVIDSON: Well, you wouldn't listen to me when I've been telling you all along to look out. Maybe I'm only an ignorant old woman, but I've lived a while longer than you have and I can see further than the end of my nose yet. You'll have to teach her a pretty sharp lesson, Jim, or, mark my words, you've not seen the end of this kind of thing. With a fellow like Clifford Osborne! There's not a girl in the district but would give him all he asked for.

She is drying her perspiring face and setting her hair right as she babbles on, heedless of the working face and trembling form of JIM.

I guess you'd better bring her back to live with me. There was none of this sort of thing when she was there. Nice goings on! Cutting up with a fellow like Osborne, with half the district looking on.

She looks around. A shaft of light cuts the darkness beyond the open door.

What's that?

Both she and JIM *hurry to look out.*

It's someone's car... turning in here. I believe it's Osborne's. Yes, it is. I'd know it anywhere. Well, what do you know about that? Driving her home! There, he's handing her out. What're they doing now? She's giving him something... no, shaking hands! Well, what d'you know about that, eh?

Hands akimbo, she turns to look at JIM. *There is that in his face that turns her malicious satisfaction into sudden alarm. She puts a hand on his arm.*

Why… Jim! What's the matter, Jim?

JIM: Let me go!

MRS DAVIDSON: [*tightening her hold*] What are you going to do? Now, don't be silly, Jim.

JIM: Let me go, I tell you. I'll show that swine… My God!… I'll show him.

He strains to get through the door.

MRS DAVIDSON: Now, Jim, wait a minute… don't do anything foolish, Jim.

He flings her aside and goes out, beside himself with passion. She hurries to the door and calls after him.

Jim! Jim! Wait a moment, Jim!

She pauses, puts a hand up to her open mouth, looks out into the darkness, gives a stifled cry of half–fear and follows after him. For a few seconds the scene remains empty, then JIM comes back into the light outside the doorway. He backs away from something that he sees before him. For a moment he pauses, unable to tear his eyes away from the sight, then he flings his hands before his eyes and staggers back into the room.

CURTAIN

Act Three

Next evening.

MRS DAVIDSON, NELLY *and* HUGHES, *a local police constable, are seated around the table.* HUGHES *is just a rough country man, ill–at–ease and very unhappy in the discharge of his duty. He is not in uniform but wears a badly fitting dark suit, with a blue shirt, open at the throat and minus a collar. He has a notebook before him and he writes in this from time to time as he hears the story of the events of the previous night.* NELLY *is still and frightened,* MRS DAVIDSON *is tearful and inclined to be hysterical, but a lot of her shrill aggressiveness has left her and, in the face of the disaster that has befallen them, she has gained almost a touch of dignity.*

HUGHES: You know I wouldn't be troubling you, Mrs Davidson, if it wasn't that I've got to, don't you?

MRS DAVIDSON: Oh, yes, constable, I know. You've been very kind and patient, but it's terrible to have to talk about these things.

HUGHES: I'll try and make it as little as I can, but you see I've got to send a report of this down to headquarters straight away.

MRS DAVIDSON: Why? They won't be sending up any of them detectives, will they?

HUGHES: [*uncomfortably*] No. You see, it won't be necessary. We know who did it.

MRS DAVIDSON: Yes. That's right.

HUGHES: But I've got to get particulars, Mrs Davidson.

MRS DAVIDSON: Well, what is it you want to know?

HUGHES: I want you to go on just from where you left off.

MRS DAVIDSON: I don't rightly remember much more. He was gone out the door before I knew what he was about and I followed after him. It was dark and I couldn't see very well, but I heard his voice calling her names… and him. Then Osborne seemed to lose his temper and I heard him swearing back… and he struck at Jim. Then Jan called out and went in between them. I couldn't see very clear as there was only the lights of the car and I was hurrying across, and the next thing I knew was when Jan began to scream… and I saw what Jim had done.

Her voice dies away and she buries her face in her hands. HUGHES *shifts his feet and writes in his book, giving her time to regain her calm.*

HUGHES: Did you see anything of this, Nelly?

NELLY: No, Mr Hughes, I wasn't there then. I was in the car with David Ritchie.

HUGHES *nods his head and turns again to* MRS DAVIDSON.

HUGHES: You say that Osborne struck him first, Mrs Davidson?

MRS DAVIDSON: That's what it looked like.

HUGHES: And he was lying on the ground when you got there?

MRS DAVIDSON: Yes, with his head against the stone. I remember that stone being there for years, long before we ever got this place. Just a bit of a thing, with a sharp point on one side.

HUGHES: Yes, I had a look at it. He was unconscious when you lifted him up?

MRS DAVIDSON: Oh yes, quite. He might have been dead but for the funny way he was breathing.

HUGHES *writes in his book and there is a little silence.*

HUGHES: I'll have to get that point clear about Osborne striking Jim first. Mrs Jim'll be able to tell about that.

MRS DAVIDSON: Goodness knows how long she will sleep. That stuff Dr Wilson gave her must be pretty strong.

HUGHES: I don't suppose she'll be much longer now. It's getting on for six o'clock.

MRS DAVIDSON: I hope not. I want to get in to see Jim some time to–night. I wonder how he is?

HUGHES: He wasn't too bad when I left. The doctor had given him something, too, but it hadn't worked with him.

MRS DAVIDSON: Oh, poor Jim!… my poor boy! Never did I think I'd see a day like this. He was such a gentle little fellow when he was a baby, constable. I remember how we used to laugh at him because he cried if anything got hurt, and I've seen him turn as sick as anything if he saw a rabbit in a trap, and now, to think that *he* should have gone and done such a dreadful thing as this!

HUGHES: I must say I find it hard to believe of Jim, myself.

MRS DAVIDSON: Doesn't it all go to show the difference a woman can make to a man? If only he'd gone and married one of our own girls, he'd never have felt like he did and nothing would have happened. He was crazy about that Jan. There's something not quite decent about a man's loving a woman the way he loved her. It isn't *good* for him!

The door behind her slowly opens and JEANNE *creeps through. She is so still and wraith–like, they do not notice her. She is dressed in her little black gown and stands leaning against the door, listening to the last vindictive sentences. She steals across to the old woman's side and holds out a hand in appeal for justice.*

JEANNE: Don't… say that!

MRS DAVIDSON: [*bewildered*] Don't say what?

Her words and sudden appearance take them all by surprise. HUGHES *gets clumsily to his feet.*

JEANNE: That the love that Jim and I 'ad was not… good. I 'ave never loved Jim so much in all my life as I love 'im now!

JEANNE'*s voice has a strange, unearthly quality. She is not yet free of the drug that has had her in its hold for many hours.*

HUGHES: Are you feeling any better, Mrs Davidson?

JEANNE: Oh, yes, I am… all right.

She seats herself at the table and looks straight in front of her. A violent shudder racks her and she recalls herself with an effort.

Won't you sit down, monsieur?

MRS DAVIDSON: You'd better get ready to go into town, Jan. Mr Hughes has been waiting to take you in.

JEANNE: [*in horror*] Waiting? To take me in?

HUGHES: No… no, it's all right, Mrs Davidson. You needn't come in unless you want to. I only want you to tell me what happened.

JEANNE: [*relaxing*] Oh!

HUGHES: You see, it's part of the necessary proceedings.

JEANNE: Yes, I suppose so.

HUGHES: [*kindly*] Just a bare outline of facts, Mrs Davidson.

JEANNE: Monsieur, can't it wait until tomorrow? I will tell you everything then. Some'ow I can't feel able to think very well to–night.

HUGHES: Well, I hardly like to do that, Mrs Davidson. You see, in a case like this...

JEANNE: It is a very dreadful case, isn't it, monsieur?

HUGHES: Yes. It certainly is.

JEANNE: And it is us! Jim and me! It cannot be true!

She seems hardly conscious of the presence of the others. She stares straight ahead and once again the violent shudder racks her.

MRS DAVIDSON: Not true? It's all too true. Jim in prison... perhaps a murderer.

JEANNE: [*springing to her feet*] No... no! It is not that... not yet! Monsieur Osborne has not died. 'E cannot die. Don't let us think of it.

MRS DAVIDSON: How can I help but think of it? It's been ringing in me ears all night. I can only see Jim as a little chap, and now, we've got to think of him as... this!

JEANNE: [*turning towards her*] Maman... mother! You and I 'ave never been to one another what we should 'ave been. Now, the man we love so much... the man we would both of us die for, is in danger and fear...

MRS DAVIDSON: Yes. And whose fault is it, I want to know?

As though she had been struck, JEANNE *drops her outstretched hand and turns away. Her eyes meet* NELLY*'s and there is a world of appeal in her glance, but* NELLY, *too, turns away.* JEANNE *wearily returns to her seat.*

JEANNE: Yes, it is my fault. I know it, and I only wish that I could take the blame.

MRS DAVIDSON: Well, that's the way in this life. The innocent always have to suffer with the guilty.

JEANNE: Murderer! Guilty! What dreadful words.

HUGHES: Now, don't you go letting yourself dwell on them too much, Mrs Davidson. Cliff Osborne is a big strong fellow and he's not dead yet, by any means.

JEANNE: [*grateful for the hint of friendliness*] Thank you, monsieur. One cannot think of Monsieur Osborne, never laughing any more, nor of Jim 'aving killed... a friend.

MRS DAVIDSON: Well, all this talking isn't going to help things. Tell Mr Hughes what he wants to know, Jan, and let's get out of this place.

JEANNE: Oh, do not ask me for that to–night. I can't tell it to–night.

MRS DAVIDSON: Why can't you? What's the matter?

JEANNE: [*dropping her head in her hands*] I am so tired... so tired!

MRS DAVIDSON: It's not a question of how you feel, but what's got to be done. Mr Hughes has been most kind waiting here for hours and wouldn't have disturbed you at any cost.

JEANNE: But I can't remember!

MRS DAVIDSON: You're still doped with that stuff the doctor gave you. Pull yourself together, Jan. It's no use giving way to things.

JEANNE *fixes her with a long, long look. Then she turns to the policeman and braces herself to meet the ordeal.*

JEANNE: Very well. What is it you want to know, monsieur?

Before he can reply, ALEXANDER RITCHIE *comes to the open door. Both* JEANNE *and* MRS DAVIDSON *get to their feet as he steps inside.* HUGHES *draws back to let him come forward, and* NELLY *remains seated.*

RITCHIE: Good afternoon.

MRS DAVIDSON: Good afternoon.

RITCHIE: I'm very sorry to hear this news, Mrs Davidson.

MRS DAVIDSON: Thank you, Mr Ritchie.

JEANNE: You... were wanting something, monsieur?

RITCHIE: [*with a glance at* HUGHES] Yes. I came out to see you on personal matters.

HUGHES: Well, I'll leave you for a while. There's several things outside I want to have a look at. Just call me when you're ready.

JEANNE: Thank you, monsieur. We will not be very long.

HUGHES *picks up his hat and goes out.*

Won't you sit down, monsieur?

RITCHIE: Thank you.

Her quiet courtesy somehow surprises him.

MRS DAVIDSON: Nelly, is that kettle boiling? Perhaps Mr Ritchie would like a cup of tea.

RITCHIE: No… no, thank you. I am not at all thirsty.

A pause. They are all waiting for him to begin. This man spells disaster for them and they are afraid of what has brought him out now.

I suppose I have no need to say what has brought me out here, Mrs Davidson?

MRS DAVIDSON: Well, no. I think we can guess. It's about… Jim?

RITCHIE: About Jim and one or two other things. I suppose you think that I am a hard man, Mrs Davidson.

MRS DAVIDSON: Well, you're not easy, Mr Ritchie, but you've always been very fair to us.

RITCHIE: I have tried to be. If ever I have done anything that may have seemed harsh, it's because I have seen that there has been nothing to be gained by doing otherwise.

MRS DAVIDSON: Yes, Mr Ritchie, but if only you knew how hard it's been to get the money we've had to pay you, when we've had to give cash for all we got at your store.

RITCHIE: Yes, I know that, Mrs Davidson, but don't misjudge me in that either. If I had not demanded cash for all you bought, can you imagine the size of the bill you would be owing me now?

She cannot answer.

Mrs Davidson, I don't want you to look upon me as an oppressor. What I have done in the past is what any businessman would have done. Against my better judgment I financed Jim in the purchase of this other property. It was neither kind nor reasonable to allow him to go getting deeper and deeper into debt when I did not see any hope of him ever doing any good.

JEANNE *has been standing a little to the back watching him, hostility and dislike on every line of her face.*

JEANNE: Could you not 'ave waited to say all this, monsieur? Do you think that we are caring very much about your money, or our money, now?

RITCHIE: [*coldly*] No, perhaps not, Mrs Davidson, but I have come out to tell you something that may interest you.

JEANNE: Then… would you… say it, monsieur!

RITCHIE: You've got a lot to face… all of you… and I want you to understand that you will have no need to worry over any money that may be due to me until Jim is back again and able to attend to things himself.

> MRS DAVIDSON *goes to speak but he motions her to silence.*

I still hold the mortgage and, when the time comes, I shall expect all the payments to be met, but, in the meantime, you can forget them.

MRS DAVIDSON: Mr Ritchie, I don't know what to say.

JEANNE: And I say that you are just a day too late, monsieur.

RITCHIE: Oh, how is that?

JEANNE: If you 'ad said this to Jim when 'e saw you yesterday, we would 'ave blessed your name. Today, you mock us. [*Losing some of her control and taking a step towards him*] Do you think that we were afraid that you would take the farms from us now? We know you far too well for that, Monsieur Ritchie! We can 'ave them now, when there's no grass and everything is dying, but, later on… when Jim is back and maybe 'as a little money, and the rain 'as come… you'll talk business then, won't you?

RITCHIE: [*dismissing what she has said as hysteria*] You do not understand.

MRS DAVIDSON: Of course she doesn't. Jan, I'm surprised at you. I think it's very good of you, Mr Ritchie, and I'm sure Jim'll say the same.

> JEANNE *turns away.* RITCHIE *looks down at the table very ill–at–ease.*

RITCHIE: There is something else I want to discuss with you. It concerns my son David, and you, Nelly.

> NELLY *is startled by the unexpectedness of the subject.*

NELLY: Yes, Mr Ritchie?

RITCHIE: I believe he has been paying you a good deal of attention lately.

NELLY: Yes, Mr Ritchie.

RITCHIE: I don't like having to say this, but under the present circumstances it might be as well for you two to see as little of one another as possible.

MRS DAVIDSON: Why... Mr Ritchie?

NELLY: [*getting to her feet*] You mean that what Jim has done may make a difference between Dave and me?

RITCHIE: I don't see how it can help doing so.

NELLY: [*scornfully*] I guess you're wrong, Mr Ritchie. It'd take more than that to come between us.

RITCHIE: I don't know how far the affair has gone, Nelly. I have heard some talk of an engagement...

NELLY: That's right. Dave has asked me to marry him.

RITCHIE: Then, in that case, I can only say that I am more than ever sorry.

MRS DAVIDSON: Mr Ritchie, whatever do you mean? What has Jim to do with Dave and Nelly?

NELLY: Have you come out here to try and get me to give up Dave?

RITCHIE: I came out to talk things over with you, Nelly.

NELLY: And does Dave know anything about this?

RITCHIE: Nothing at all.

NELLY: [*slowly shaking her head*] Then you can say all you like. I'd never give him up till he asks me to himself.

RITCHIE: [*rising to his feet and taking up his hat*] If that is the case, it is no use my saying any more.

JEANNE: Put that down!

They all look at her in astonishment.

You are not going off like that. Do you think you can spoil the 'appiness of two people and then go off without a word of explanation? Why is Nelly not to marry your son?

NELLY: I know why. You've never taken any notice of me; you've never even spoken to me any more than you can help. Don't think I haven't noticed it. You've thought all along that I wasn't good enough for Dave and now you've got something real against me and you're going to make the most of it.

RITCHIE: Up to this, I had nothing against you. I have been a poor man, Nelly. All I have, I have worked for and worked hard, and for nearly thirty years I have had only one view in mind—to see my son happily and comfortably settled, with a family to carry on my name and enjoy what I have earned.

NELLY: Well?

JEANNE: Monsieur Ritchie, why don't you say what is in your mind? Why don't you say that Nelly is the sister of a man in gaol, and so you don't want any more of 'er?

RITCHIE: I say no such thing, but, with the sister of a man capable of doing what Jim has done, there is a certain amount of risk, and I don't want my son to take that risk.

JEANNE: In other words, you feel that Nelly 'as a… taint?

NELLY: Mr Ritchie, that's not fair.

MRS DAVIDSON: How can you say such a thing, Jan?

RITCHIE: Those are not my words, Nelly, but to a certain degree I think they may be right.

JEANNE: You do? And do you know what I think?…

MRS DAVIDSON: Jan! Will you be quiet? Don't listen to her, Mr Ritchie.

JEANNE: No, I will not be quiet. I 'ave listen long enough to what this man 'as got to say.

RITCHIE: Mrs Davidson, I think this matter concerns Nelly.

JEANNE: This matter concerns Jim and me and Jim's mother as much as it does anybody else? You 'ave stood up there and told Nelly she is not fit to be a mother, not fit to be a wife. Are we to say nothing at all?

NELLY: Is that what you meant?

JEANNE: Of course it's what 'e meant… only you could not see it.

NELLY: You mean… you mean… because Jim did that to Clifford Osborne, I'm not any good any more?

RITCHIE: The best thing that can be said for Jim is that he did it in a fit of temporary insanity.

NELLY: Jim? Insane?

MRS DAVIDSON: How can you say such a thing, Mr Ritchie?

RITCHIE: Wasn't there a time, Mrs Davidson, when your son was confined in a mental hospital?

MRS DAVIDSON: That was in the war, and no wonder he was there after all he'd gone through.

RITCHIE: Every other man who was at the war had to go through it, too.

Most of them came out all right, the ones with the weakness gave way. Jim has been under a strain again… and he has been unable to stand it.

MRS DAVIDSON: Mr Ritchie, Jim's as right as you or me!

RITCHIE: Perhaps he is, but your son has attempted the life of a fellow man. If that man should die he may have to stand his trial on a charge of murder. If he did it when in full possession of his senses, knowing what he did… I am very sorry for you all!

They shrink from the truth in his words.

JEANNE: Monsieur Ritchie, are you not satisfied? 'Ave you not already brought enough misery to us without you must say that?

NELLY: Misery! Who's been the cause of all this but you? Do you see what you've done, you and your Osborne? I wish to God I'd never seen you.

JEANNE: Nelly!

NELLY: I do. If you hadn't have gone on the way you did, none of this would have happened.

JEANNE: Oh, Nelly! What are you saying?

NELLY: What we're all of us thinking. There's no–one, knowing everything, who would wonder at Jim doing what he did.

> JEANNE *looks at her aghast, refusing to grasp what her words imply.*

RITCHIE: Don't you think it would be better if we left the discussion of all this till some other time? I feel sure, Nelly, that when you come to think things over camly, you will see what I ask of you is the right thing to do.

JEANNE: [*impulsively*] Ah, monsieur, is separating two people who really love each other ever the right thing to do? [*Crossing the room and laying a hand on his arm*] Do not make me feel that I 'ave done this terrible thing to David and Nelly as well as what I 'ave done to myself.

> NELLY *dries her tears and she and her mother gaze in something like astonishment.* RITCHIE *opens his mouth to speak but* JEANNE *forestalls him.*

Just say that you will wait a little longer before you speak to him.

Nelly 'as need of 'er lover now, monsieur. It is when sadness comes that people love each other most, you know.

RITCHIE *has no reply for this and, in the little pause that follows,* DR WILSON *steps into the doorway. He hesitates a moment, then comes in, followed by* HUGHES.

WILSON: Well, how are you all feeling now?

RITCHIE: Good day, Wilson.

WILSON *nods in reply.*

MRS DAVIDSON: Oh, doctor, my head's something cruel.

RITCHIE: Have you come from town, doctor?

WILSON: Yes.

MRS DAVIDSON: Any... news?

She asks this fearfully. WILSON *bites his lip and glances across at* JEANNE *who is watching him with an agony of appeal in her eyes.*

WILSON: Yes. Clifford Osborne died this afternoon.

JEANNE: Ah, no! No!

She holds a side of her head in either hand and staggers slightly. WILSON *steps swiftly to her side and helps her to a chair.* MRS DAVIDSON *and* NELLY *cling to one another.*

MRS DAVIDSON: Died! Oh, my goodness me!

RITCHIE: [*to* WILSON] This is a bad business. Did he regain consciousness?

WILSON: No, just a collapse.

MRS DAVIDSON: Oh, what are we going to do now? What are we going to do?

HUGHES: [*kindly*] Now then, Mrs Davidson, don't go upsetting yourself like that.

MRS DAVIDSON: If only we could do something to help Jim. But we've had to sit and wait all day, wondering and wondering, and now there's still nothing for us to do.

WILSON: The best thing that you can do is to go home and try and get some rest.

You've been up all night, you know, and you must be done up.

MRS DAVIDSON: There won't be much sleep for me to–night.

WILSON: Well, Nelly, you see that she goes to bed and don't let her go wearing herself out when she can rest.

NELLY: Yes, doctor.

> MRS RYAN *bustles up to the doorway. She hesitates uncertainly when she sees who is there.*

MRS RYAN: Oh, goodness me, I'd no idea there'd be so many here.

WILSON: Come in, Mrs Ryan.

MRS RYAN: I just thought I'd pop in to see if there was anything that we could do for you.

MRS DAVIDSON: Oh… have you heard?

MRS RYAN: Yes. I heard it in town and I made Ryan turn round and bring me right out here. 'Now's the time to let them know that they've got neighbours,' I says, and out we came. So, if there's anything that we can do for you, you say the word and Tom and I'll do it, and glad to.

MRS DAVIDSON: Oh, no. There's nothing to be done.

MRS RYAN: Now, yes there is. I've been too long on a farm to swallow that. I saw some washing on your lines as I was coming past and what about the fowls? You come along with me and get your mind off worrying. What do you say, doctor?

WILSON: I think you're right, Mrs Ryan. A little work in time of trouble does a lot of good.

MRS RYAN: That's just what I says. My, my dear, I remember the nights I couldn't sleep just after Jessie went. Many's the time I've got up in the middle of the night and scrubbed out the kitchen or done a bit of washing, just to ease myself. We get our troubles, all of us, and it's the ones that gets theirs first that knows what helps. Now, come along, now. You and Nelly get your hats on and we'll go across and do what's wanting to be done and then you'll both come over and stop the night with me, and, in the morning, things won't look so bad.

> MRS RYAN *pats the back of the weeping mother. Blind with tears, the old woman gets to her feet, gropes for the hand of her comforter and reaches for her hat.*

RITCHIE: I'll be going in a minute, Mrs Ryan. Could I drive you across?

MRS RYAN: Well, that's kind of you, Mr Ritchie. We'd be grateful if you would.

RITCHIE: Very well, I'll bring the car round to the front.

He takes up his hat.

MRS RYAN: We'll be ready in a jiffy.

RITCHIE: Don't hurry. Good–bye, Wilson. Good day, Hughes.

WILSON & HUGHES: [*together*] Good–bye, Mr Ritchie.

Exit RITCHIE. MRS DAVIDSON *dries her eyes and turns towards* JEANNE.

MRS DAVIDSON: I suppose Jeanne had best be coming with us.

WILSON: I'll look after Jeanne, Mrs Davidson. She's coming in with us. Mrs Wilson sent an invitation that can't be refused and it's better for her to be near Jim.

MRS DAVIDSON: Well, I want to get into town, too. I must see Jim to–night.

WILSON: When I came out Jim was asleep and I left word that he was not to be disturbed or told anything till I got back, so if you come in tomorrow morning it'll be time enough.

MRS DAVIDSON: [*drearily, no longer able to assert herself*] Oh, very well then, I suppose there's nothing to be done but get home. [*She trails towards the door, pausing close to* JEANNE] Now, pull yourself together, Jan. It's no good giving way to things. Nelly and I have got to suffer just as much as you have, and it's worse for us, because we've done nothing.

JEANNE *does not move.*

WILSON: [*his fingers on her pulse*] She'll be all right in a little while. Just leave her to me.

MRS DAVIDSON: All right, doctor. We'll see you tomorrow, then. You're ready, Mrs Ryan, aren't you?

MRS RYAN: Yes, I'm ready.

MRS DAVIDSON *and* NELLY *go out of the door.* MRS RYAN *stops and looks compassionately at* JEANNE.

Poor little girl! Life's been sort of hard on her, somehow.

JEANNE *does not stir. The doctor nods his head in silence.* MRS RYAN *sighs and goes towards the door.*

So long, Bob.

HUGHES: Good–bye, Mrs Ryan.

She goes out of the door. WILSON *now takes up his small black bag and sets it on the table. Out of it he takes a phial and pours some liquid into a cup. He dips some water out of the kerosene bucket, pours it in and goes across to* JEANNE.

WILSON: [*loudly and clearly*] Take this, will you, Jeanne?

JEANNE *glances up and takes it without a word. After she has drunk it, she sinks back into her old apathetic attitude.* WILSON *and* HUGHES *watch her anxiously.*

HUGHES: Doesn't look too clever, does she?

WILSON: Judging by her pulse, it's not surprising.

HUGHES: Perhaps I'd better let her alone for a while.

WILSON: What do you want with her?

HUGHES: I've got to get a statement from her some time today.

WILSON: Well, you've got no hope of getting it at present. This girl's in no fit state for further strain.

HUGHES: Well, if you say so, doctor, that makes it all right.

WILSON: Give her a chance to pull herself together. She'll probably be all right in half an hour or so.

HUGHES: Right–oh! Just as you say. [*Looking around the room*] I wonder where she keeps her buckets?

WILSON: What on earth do you want a bucket for?

HUGHES: Well, I noticed that the cows haven't been milked today and I thought, perhaps, while I was waiting…

He is a simple, somewhat loutish fellow, and looks enquiringly at the doctor.

WILSON: That's a good idea. Here, take this and empty the water out. Goodness knows where things are.

He takes up the kerosene bucket.

HUGHES: Good–oh!

WILSON: I'll see how she feels about having a talk to you and give you a call if she is up to it.

HUGHES: Good–oh! I'll be outside then.

After HUGHES *has gone out, the doctor seats himself near* JEANNE. *He takes out his pipe, lights it and watches her. The very silence rouses her and she looks around.*

JEANNE: 'As everybody gone?

WILSON: Everybody.

JEANNE *gives a long sigh and there is another silence.*

JEANNE: What... 'appened?

WILSON: Nothing. He just died.

JEANNE: Never spoke?

WILSON: No. He was just as you saw him; then he suddenly stopped breathing.

JEANNE: 'Ow dreadful. To think that he could go so easily.

She sits up and rests her head in her hands.

WILSON: How are you feeling, now?

JEANNE: Sick.

Her reply is so natural and so unexpected, WILSON *can scarcely repress a smile.*

WILSON: That's the morphia. It'll wear off in a while.

JEANNE: [*desperately*] Oh, if I could only make myself understand! But I cannot realise. Why, only yesterday 'e was standing 'ere... alive... 'ere in this room, laughing with me, and now! Oh, I cannot think that I will never 'ear 'im laugh again! [*Her voice breaks and she bites her quivering lip*] Thoughts keep running round and round in my 'ead... I cannot realise this is true.

WILSON: Don't try, Jeanne.

JEANNE: Why is it we can never see into tomorrow, so that we could know the dreadful things that can 'appen because of the thoughtless little things we do today?

WILSON: And what did you do yesterday, Jeanne?

JEANNE: That's just it, doctor. I cannot think of anything that I 'ave ever done to bring on such a thing as this.

WILSON: Was Jim ever jealous of Osborne?

JEANNE: [*spreading her hands*] Jim was jealous of everyone, doctor.

WILSON: [*leaning forward*] What do you mean, jealous of everyone?

JEANNE: Well, you see... when I first met Jim... you know 'ow it was in Paree, when the war was on... no–one knowing when the end would come... for all of us?

WILSON: Yes, I know.

JEANNE: In Paree, some'ow, no–one seem to think of things the way they do out here. Everybody think of being 'appy, to get as much of life and what was sweet in life, while there was still time.

She pauses, searching his face to see if she can go on. In the kindly tolerance of his expression she is reassured.

I do not 'ave to tell you any more. But Jim never seem to forget that when I see 'im... and I love 'im... that is enough. I know the things that 'e 'as come from. 'E is tired, and afraid, and did not know the ways of women. Oh, there were so many things to make me love 'im, doctor, and I try, with my love, to shut away the memory of all the things that 'e 'as seen, and suffered. And could I ever 'ave done that if I 'ad let 'im kiss me... and then sent 'im away... to spend the night alone?

She again searches his face for understanding and is not disappointed.

WILSON: And Jim has thought that... what you could give to him... you could give to others?

JEANNE: Yes, that is it.

WILSON: Oh, Jeanne... my dear, my dear, why did you do it?

JEANNE: Do what, doctor?

WILSON: Go to that stupid dance!

JEANNE: [*springing to her feet*] Oh, do not ask me that! That is what I keep saying all the time. Why did I do it? I didn't like it. I was un'appy there all the time and that is why I ask Monsieur Osborne to bring me 'ome again when it was only 'alf past ten. Nelly is right. Everywhere I look I see that she is right. It is my fault, all of it. If only I 'ad not done this thing... and that thing... nothing would 'ave 'appened. Oh, why didn't you let me die one of those times and save us all?

WILSON: Steady... steady now, lass. You mustn't let yourself go like that.

Under his touch and the sound of his voice she grows calm again.

JEANNE: Yes, I know. But if only I could do something, anything, to undo the terrible thing that I 'ave done!

WILSON: Now listen to me. It's ridiculous for you to go taking all the blame like this. You may have been a little foolish, but you have nothing more to reproach yourself with than that.

JEANNE: Oh, yes, I 'ave, doctor. I should never 'ave gone away and left Jim last night. 'E was not fit to be left alone, and I knew it.

WILSON: Why? Wasn't he... well?

JEANNE: Jim 'as not been well for some time.

WILSON: Has he been having any trouble with his head?

JEANNE: Yes.

WILSON: Why didn't he come to see me about it?

JEANNE: 'E never would, doctor. 'E seemed to be afraid of what you would say.

WILSON: Poor devil!

JEANNE: Poor Jim! Oh, doctor, what is going to 'appen to 'im now? They could not 'ang a man for doing what 'e 'as done?

WILSON: Oh, no. Jim's in no danger of being hanged.

JEANNE: Then, gaol? Will they put 'im in gaol?

WILSON: I can't say about that, Jeanne, but I should think that the fact of Jim once having been a nerve case should help a good deal.

JEANNE: What difference does that make?

WILSON: Well, it's hardly fair to judge him like other men.

JEANNE: Oh, don't say that! That is the worst thing you could possibly say... to Jim!

WILSON: But why?

JEANNE: Because, ever since that time, Jim 'as felt that... 'e is not quite the same as other men. I 'ave never spoke to anyone before, but always Jim 'as been afraid that one day it would come back to 'im and 'e might do something, like 'e 'as done.

WILSON: Good God!

JEANNE: Do you know, deep down inside I feel that Jim 'as been glad that there 'as never been a child come 'ome to us?

WILSON: Jeanne, that's a terrible thing.

JEANNE: It is a terrible thing, doctor.

WILSON: But what are you going to do? The old history is bound to be brought up. There's no other explanation possible.

JEANNE: You think that Jim was… bad again when 'e did it?

WILSON: Temporarily… yes.

JEANNE: [*in despair*] That is what everyone will think. I can only see that it is because Jim loves me so much. I am all 'e 'as in life, without me 'e could not go on, and 'e felt that Monsieur Osborne might be trying to take me from 'im and 'e struck at 'im…

WILSON: [*struck by a sudden thought*] Jeanne!

JEANNE: Yes, doctor?

WILSON: There never was any cause for Jim feeling like he did about Osborne, was there?

> JEANNE *hardly comprehends.*

You know what I mean… Oh, Lord, I know there wasn't.

JEANNE: What did you mean then, doctor? Why did you ask?

WILSON: Just for the moment the thought came to me, forgive me, Jeanne, that Jim may not have been so much to blame after all.

JEANNE: *What* did you say?

WILSON: Jeanne, I didn't say it. It was gone the moment I thought it.

JEANNE: But you said, 'Jim may not 'ave been so much to blame after all'. What did you mean by that?

WILSON: My dear, I didn't mean it.

JEANNE: Answer me! What did you mean?

WILSON: Well, if there had ever been any cause for Jim's going for Osborne about you…

JEANNE: You would not 'ave blamed 'im?

WILSON: Well, I could have understood it.

JEANNE: Jim would 'ave acted… as any other man would 'ave done?

WILSON: Well, frankly… yes.

JEANNE: Oh God! 'Elp me to think! 'Elp me to think!

WILSON: [*alarmed*] Jeanne, what is it?

JEANNE: I don't know. [*Walking about the room*] It would be so easy… so easy!

WILSON: What would be so easy?

JEANNE: To make them believe what they are everyone of them thinking.

WILSON: [*beginning to understand*] Jeanne, what are you talking about?

JEANNE: The way to undo… what I 'ave done.

WILSON: But you're crazy! You don't mean…

JEANNE: I do! Jim will be judged by men, won't 'e? And what man will blame 'im… if I tell the truth?

WILSON: The truth? The truth?

JEANNE *looks him straight between the eyes.*

Jeanne, I don't believe you.

JEANNE: Then, I must be a better liar next time, doctor.

WILSON: But you can't! Think of the future.

JEANNE: Think of the future if I don't do it. This may give me Jim— save 'im. Five years in gaol are better than one year in that dreadful place they call a mental 'ospital and, if I'm very clever… there will not be gaol.

WILSON: [*taking her hands*] Jeanne, you'll never do it. You'll never be able to lie about a thing of this kind.

JEANNE: Oh yes, I will and, what is more, there is no–one who will doubt. Is there anyone, from Jim's mother to the last man and woman in this place, who is not already thinking it? They 'ave been waiting for this kind of thing for years and now it 'as come.

WILSON: I can't stand by and see you do this thing.

JEANNE: You can't prevent me. It's my one chance of 'appiness and I've got to take it.

WILSON: That it should be necessary for you to do such a thing!

JEANNE: No–one dies of broken 'earts, doctor, and Jim and I will get on… some'ow. There is always this, all through the good and bad, no matter what 'as 'appened, Jim and I 'ave loved each other.

WILSON: I suppose so, and in the end, that may be the only thing that matters.

There is a little silence before JEANNE *braces herself for further ordeal and glances out of the door.*

JEANNE: That good Monsieur Hughes must be tired of waiting for me.

WILSON: Hughes? I'd forgotten all about him.

JEANNE: Will you go and tell 'im I am… ready to begin?

WILSON: Are you certain of yourself?

JEANNE: Quite certain.

WILSON: Be very careful what you tell him, Jeanne. Everything you say must be absolutely convincing or else it will be no use at all.

JEANNE: It will be convincing.

She moves wearily over to the table as the doctor goes towards the door. Suddenly a thought comes to her and she stands perfectly still, her face upraised.

'If there's ever anything that I can do to make things easier for you, you know you've only got to say the word, don't you?' [*Her voice breaks*] Oh, Monsieur Osborne… my friend… my friend… I 'ave killed you and now I must damn you. You and me together!

WILSON: [*crossing to her side*] Jeanne, Jeanne, this is a terrible thing that you are going to do. Are you sure that you can go through with it?

JEANNE: [*magnificently*] I can go through with anything. Am I not a Frenchwoman?

WILSON: [*with a sigh*] Very well, then. Will you be all right here alone while I go out and get Hughes?

JEANNE: [*wildly*] Alone? 'Ow else should I be but alone? I've got to be alone always… always!

She leans her head on her arm and bursts into a storm of weeping.

WILSON: Jeanne, this is so bad for you.

He is helpless in the face of her terrible despair. After a moment he picks up his hat, glances out of the door and turns back to JEANNE. *There is infinite compassion on his face and he picks up one of her little, toil–marred hands and pats it gently. Then he lays it back on the table and goes slowly out.* JEANNE's *desperate sobbing dies and she rises to her feet, turning mechanically about the room. Coming to a halt before the stove, she sees that the fire is out. She picks up a poker and commences to stir it, but realisation returns to her and she drops it with a little whimper of distress. She turns away and sees* HARRY *come to the door.*

JEANNE: [*with a wan little smile*] Well… 'Arry!

HARRY: I just thought I'd come along to see how you was gettin' along, Mis' Davidson.

JEANNE: Oh, I am… all right, 'Arry.

HARRY: I say… Hughes has been puttin' it across me out there… I had to tell him what I heard last night when I brought that bit of ice. I hope it won't make no difference to Jim.

JEANNE: Oh, no... it won't make any difference, 'Arry; it might even 'elp.

HARRY: I'm glad of that.

An unhappy little pause.

[*Suddenly*] Here's a parcel for you, Mis' Davidson. I got it at the post office as I come along.

JEANNE: A parcel? For me?

HARRY: Yes. Here you are.

She takes it listlessly and puts it on the table. Picking up a knife, she cuts the string and opens it. As she draws aside the tissue paper and sees what it contains, she gives a cry of pain. It is the set of silk lingerie. Half instinctively she lifts them to her face, then realising the irony, she lets them drop. HARRY watches with wide, uncomprehending eyes. Then, through the silence, comes a slow patter on the iron roof. They both stiffen into attention and hold their breath.

Listen! Rain! It's raining!

The sound grows louder and more distinct. He rushes out, leaving her alone.

JEANNE: [*broken, beaten*] Rain!

THE END

Appendix

The 1973 Revision (A)

The following extracts from the recently revised version of The Touch of Silk (referred to as A, and discussed by Professor A.D. Hope in his preface to the play, published separately) will perhaps give the reader an indication of the extent and direction of the revision.

ACT ONE

The following illustrates the different feel of the social interchange in the shop. The spareness of stage directions is worthy of note, especially as regards the first appearance of Ritchie—gone are the thumbnail sketches of 1942. Some idea of the detailed reordering of events in this act may be gained by seeking out the equivalents in the main text.

A   CLIFF OSBORNE *returns, carrying several rolls of material.*

MRS RYAN: There you are at last, Cliff. I thought you'd gone for good.
CLIFF: Sorry, Mrs Ryan.
MRS DAVIDSON: Well, if it isn't Cliff Osborne!
CLIFF: Mrs Davidson! This is a surprise!

> *He puts down the rolls of silk and takes her hands.*

MRS RYAN: This is the first time you've seen him?
MRS DAVIDSON: Yes. I heard that he was here but didn't know he'd got his old job back. Cliff, you're looking fine.
CLIFF: So are you, you haven't changed a bit.
MRS DAVIDSON: Get along with you. Nelly, come here. You remember Cliff.
CLIFF: Is this really Nelly? You were only that high when I saw you last.

> NELLY *giggles.*

MRS DAVIDSON: Quite the young lady, isn't she?

CLIFF: She certainly is. I don't suppose she even remembers me.

NELLY: Yes I do. You used to have a motorbike and took me for a ride on the back.

CLIFF: And you didn't like putting your arms around my waist and hanging on.

MRS RYAN: She's got over that!

CLIFF: Where's old Jim?

MRS DAVIDSON: He's with Ritchie, he'll be here soon. My, but it's good to see you, Cliff.

CLIFF: I hear he got married since I've been away.

MRS DAVIDSON: Oh yes—he got married. To a French girl.

CLIFF: You're kidding! Good old Jim! How did he manage that?

MRS DAVIDSON: One of them war romances. Met her when he was on leave in Paris.

CLIFF: That so?

MRS DAVIDSON: Yes. Well, I've got things to do. Come out and see us some time, Cliff.

CLIFF: I'll fix that up with Jim.

MRS DAVIDSON: You get what you want, Mrs Ryan, and we'll have a bit of lunch together afterwards.

MRS RYAN: Suits me fine. Nell, you come and help me pick out something nice for Jessie.

> *The light fades and a single spot picks up* JIM *and* RITCHIE *on the extreme left. An upended packing case serves* RITCHIE *for a seat while* JIM *stands, rather nervously rolling a cigarette.*

RITCHIE: But Ed's let the place go to the pack. It needs new fences and a windmill and you'll have to restock it…

JIM: I know that, Mr Ritchie. It's going to take quite a lot of money to get it going. On the other hand, Ed's willing to sell cheap.

RITCHIE: Ed's a fool. When his father died it was one of the pick places in the district.

JIM: Ed never was cut out to be a farmer.

RITCHIE: He's bone lazy, that's his trouble.

JIM: Perhaps he'll do better in the city. He's talking of setting up in business somewhere.

RITCHIE: I wish him luck with that! But what makes you think you'll make a better fist of it than Ed?

JIM: For one thing, I'm not lazy.

RITCHIE: No, I'll give you that.

JIM: So, what about it? Are you prepared to stake me, or aren't you?

RITCHIE: Hold your horses, Jim, these things can't be done in a hurry. What does your mother think about it?

JIM: Oh, you know her. Once you sign a mortgage you're halfway to the workhouse.

RITCHIE: She's one of the few people in this district who's never been in debt. I take off my hat to her.

JIM: So do I. But the truth is, Mr Ritchie, she and Jeanne don't hit it off too well. It's no–one's fault, but Jeanne and I have got to have a place of our own.

RITCHIE: Even a tumbledown place like Ed's?

JIM: It isn't all that bad.

RITCHIE: I think I see your point, Jim.

JIM: Do you? But it's not the only reason. I don't want to be a small–time cocky all my life and the old farm just isn't big enough to bring in more than a bare living. If I get this place of Ed's I've got a chance of coming good.

RITCHIE: Got ambitions, have you, Jim?

JIM: Why not? With a bit of luck and one or two good seasons…

RITCHIE: Yes, a few good seasons. We've had good rains for the past four years, but suppose your luck runs out?

JIM: That's the gamble.

RITCHIE: And you're willing to stake everything you've got on it.

JIM: Hell, a man has got to take a risk some time. Haven't you?

RITCHIE: Not often.

JIM: And I'm not asking you to take a risk now. You'll have good security for your money, and you know it. So, make up your mind. If you're not interested, say the word, and I'll go to the bank.

RITCHIE: And they'll give you what you want, the same as I will if you're absolutely set on it.

JIM: You will!

RITCHIE: Why not? As you say, there's good security.

JIM: Then what have you been arguing about?

RITCHIE: It was my duty to point out the risks.

JIM: Don't think I don't know about the risks. I've weighed them up and reckon that, with luck, I'll make the grade.

RITCHIE: You're going to need it, Jim.

JIM: Don't we all? You've been lucky in your time.

RITCHIE: What gives you that idea?

JIM: Starve the crows, you own half Quamby!

Blackout. The lights go up on the main scene. No–one has changed position and they pick up the dialogue where they left off.

MRS DAVIDSON: What do you suggest, Stel?

STELLA: M–m–m, let me see. It's the one you bought for Janet Dawson's wedding, isn't it?

MRS DAVIDSON: And she's just had her third.

STELLA: Why not have a new one? We've got some lovely hats this year.

And so on. The following brief scene is added after the curtain falls on the scene in the shop:

A   *Total darkness. The sound of a dreamy waltz being played.* NELLY *and* DAVE RITCHIE *are lit by a spot as they dance slowly in front of the curtain. He holds her very close.*

DAVE: Get this into your silly little head, will you? It won't make the slightest difference.

NELLY: But, Dave, it must. You'll be away for months and you'll meet other girls.

DAVE: What if I do?

NELLY: You'll forget all about me.

DAVE: As far as I'm concerned, there aren't any other girls. There never have been.

NELLY: That's how you feel now, but when you get to London and New York…

DAVE: [*stopping to take her by both shoulders*] Now, listen to me. If I'm so weak–willed that I can't stand up to that, I'm not worth having.

NELLY: [*with her arms around him*] Yes, you are. I'd have you, Dave, no matter what you did, as long as you still wanted me.

DAVE: I'll be wanting you.

They dance again.

NELLY: I'm such a small–town girl, and you'll be meeting…

DAVE: Duchesses and movie stars, all fighting to get hold of me.

NELLY: Don't make fun of me.

DAVE: I will, if you insist on being silly.

NELLY: Dave, I love you so. I just can't bear the thought of not seeing you.

DAVE: It's only six months. I'll write to you and think of you.

NELLY: Will you, Dave? Promise!

DAVE: And when I get back we'll see how the old man takes to the idea of us getting married.

NELLY: Married! Do you mean that? *Really?*

DAVE: Sure, I do. What else?

NELLY: Dave—Oh, Dave!

She hides her face against his shoulder.

DAVE: Here! What's the matter?

NELLY: I never thought you'd want to marry me.

DAVE: Why not?

NELLY: You never said… and I'm so ordinary.

DAVE: Listen! Any more of that and I'll change my mind. You're my girl, see? The one I'm going to marry, and she isn't any ordinary girl. Got that?

NELLY: [*enraptured*] Yes.

He kisses her very tenderly.

DAVE: You're my girl, for keeps. You understand?

NELLY: For keeps.

The music swells and the lights fade.

ACT TWO

This act is without any major structural change. However, the detailed rewriting is at times sufficiently radical to indicate a change of concept. For instance, while sexual malaise is present in 1942—at times with a surprising frankness—there is a prevailing decorum of both language and action which develops into a poignant innocence in the offstage handshake at the end of Act Two. In A, this decorum has been eroded generally, the handshake is gone, and as a result Jeanne's relationship with Osborne is not as unambiguously platonic. The actualities of the play are less clearcut. The act now ends as follows.

A   MRS DAVIDSON: Gone to the fancy dress ball! What have you got to say to that, Jim? A pretty lot of fools we're going to look when it gets about that we've been tearing round the district looking for her.

JIM: Be quiet, ma.

MRS DAVIDSON: Why should I? It'd pay you to listen to me now and again. I'll bet this was all fixed up between her and Cliff this afternoon.

JIM: Just go, will you?

MRS DAVIDSON: Not till I've had my say. You're a fool, Jim. Maybe I'm only an ignorant old woman, but I can see a good deal further than the end of my nose.

JIM: Be quiet, do you hear?

His voice is steadily rising.

MRS DAVIDSON: You wouldn't listen when I warned you about letting him come here so often. Just an old friend of the family! Funny thing, he never bothered to call in and say hello to me!

JIM: Ma! I've had enough. Just go! Get out of here and say no more.

MRS DAVIDSON: I'll say plenty, and you'd better listen. [*Seeing the expression on* JIM*'s face*] Jim, what's wrong?

JIM: Nothing. Go away!

MRS DAVIDSON: You're shaking, Jim. Sit down and let me get you something.

She takes his arm. He shakes her off.

JIM: Damn you, leave me alone! Get away, I tell you!

MRS DAVIDSON: Jim, don't speak to me like that.

The beam of car headlights sweeps through the door, followed by the sound of a motor. They both turn around.

That's someone's car. [*Looking out the door*] It's Osborne's, coming in the gate, I'd know it anywhere. Well, of all the nerve.

She turns to look at JIM. *His face is convulsed with anger.*

Jim! Now, listen, Jim…

He thrusts her aside and moves into the doorway, staring at what he sees outside.

Take it easy, Jim, don't lose your head. Just listen to me, Jim

JIM: Shut up!

He glances at the knife beside the door, half lifting his hand. She seizes his arm.

MRS DAVIDSON: Jim! For God's sake, no! Not that!

He frees himself so roughly that she staggers back into the room. Before she can recover herself, he has gone out the door. She runs after him.

Jim! Jim, boy! Come back… come back…

She disappears into the night. The sound of angry voices breaks the silence, then JEANNE's *voice rises above the rest.*

JEANNE: Jim! Oh God! Oh no!

MRS DAVIDSON: [*a long–drawn cry*] Jim–m–m–m!

From ACT THREE

Constable Hughes is written out of the play, being replaced in his neighbourly role by Mrs Ryan, and in his official capacity by the offstage police. Jeanne's entrance is significantly different, in that Mrs Davidson's malicious comments are more explicitly related to sexual matters. The opposition between the two women is in a way simplified.

A   MRS DAVIDSON: She's the one who should be locked up in that cell, not Jim.

NELLY: Oh, ma!

MRS DAVIDSON: He was a good quiet boy till she got hold of him, and Cliff was his friend, like brothers they were, and look what she's done to both of them.

They are not aware that JEANNE *has opened the bedroom door*

and overhears.

MRS RYAN: I must say she had no business going to that dance.

MRS DAVIDSON: That's only half of it. There's been trouble all along. I knew what Jim was in for, right from the start.

MRS RYAN: My, she was a pretty little thing then. All the same, I remember saying to Ryan I didn't see how she was going to settle down out here.

MRS DAVIDSON: Doesn't it show the difference a woman can make to a man? If only Jim had married one of our own girls none of this would've happened. He was crazy about that Jan; and the things that went on when they first got married!

MRS RYAN: [*avid for details*] What sort of things?

MRS DAVIDSON: Well you may ask! Their room was next to mine, and I had to cover my head with the pillow so that I wouldn't hear.

NELLY: Hear what, ma?

MRS DAVIDSON: I wouldn't like to say. But I'll tell you this much, there were times when they were not much better than a pair of animals!

JEANNE: How can you say such cruel things?

MRS DAVIDSON: [*recovering from her surprise*] I'm saying what I know.

The Touch of Silk, Melbourne 1942. First produced The Play–house, Melbourne 1928.

The Touch of Silk, anonymously adapted for radio, 1938. First produced 3AR Melbourne 1938. MS. in ABC script library, Sydney.

The Touch of Silk, a revision by Betty Roland set in the mid–'fifties, c. 1955. Unproduced. MS. in possession of author.

The Touch of Silk, a further revision, c. 1973, Produced in work–shop by Melbourne Theatre Company, 1974. MS. in possession of author.

OTHER PLAYS

Morning, in *Best Australian One–Act Plays*, ed. William Moore and T. I. Moore, Sydney 1937. First produced Kiosk Theatre, Fawkner Park, Melbourne 1932.

The Gate of Bronze, a fantasy. First produced The Hermitage Church of England Girls' Grammar School, Geelong 1925. MS. in possession of author.

Are You Ready, Comrade?, a political drama. First produced Patch Theatre, Perth 1937. MS. in possession of New Theatre, Sydney.

Madame Bovary, adapted from Flaubert's novel. First produced Independent Theatre, Sydney 1946. MS. in possession of Independent Theatre.

Don Quixote de la Mancha, adapted from Cervantes' novel, Unproduced. MSS. in Campbell Howard collection, University of New England Library, and in the National Library, Canberra.

Granite Peak, a drama. Unproduced, MS. in possession of author. TV adaptation by Betty Roland produced for BBC, London 1952. MS. in possession of author.

The First Gentleman, radio play. First produced 3AR Melbourne 1945, MS. in ABC script library, Sydney.

Daddy Was Asleep, radio play. First produced 2BL Sydney 1945. MS. in possession of author.

New Day, adaptation for radio of *Morning*. First produced 3AR Melbourne 1945. MS. in ABC script library, Sydney.

The White Cockade, radio serial in 62 episodes. First produced Lux Radio Theatre. Date? No MS. traced.

A Woman Scorned, radio play. First produced Lux Radio Theatre, Date? No MS. traced,

NOVELS

The Other Side of Sunset, London 1972.
No Ordinary Man, London 1974.

CHILDREN'S BOOKS

The Forbidden Bridge, London 1961.
Jamie's Discovery, London 1963.
Jamie's Summer Visitor, London 1964.
Jamie's Other Grandmother, London 1965.
The Bush Bandits, Melbourne 1966.

OTHER PUBLICATIONS

Lesbos: the Pagan Island, Melbourne 1963.
Sydney in Colour and Black and White, Sydney 1965.

WRITINGS ON BETTY ROLAND

Green, H. M., *A History of Australian Literature*, Sydney 1961, Vol. 2, pp. 112–113,

Rees. Leslie, *The Making of Australian Drama*, Sydney 1973, pp. 186–189.

Notes

1. Jamie, the eponymous hero of four of the children's books, lives with his mother on an uncle's property in the Goulburn Valley. *The Touch of Silk* is of course set in the Mallee district.
2. The Melbourne Repertory Theatre was founded by Gregan McMahon in 1910. The policy of this amateur theatrical group was to make good the neglect of the commercial managements by presenting serious drama from Europe (Shaw, Ibsen, Chekhov, etc.) and also some Australian plays. It continued to perform this function after its charismatic founder moved on to work for the Tait brothers in commercial theatre.
3. Frank D. Clewlow, an actor with experience in British repertory theatre, came to Australia in the nineteen tens to work for Alan Wilkie's Shakespearean company. He became director of the Melbourne Repertory Theatre in 1928 and later joined the ABC as radio play producer. He was appointed Federal Controller of Programmes in 1936 when that office was established, and continued to produce plays for the ABC in Tasmania after his retirement from office in the early nineteen fifties. The most notable of his productions for radio was the original broadcast of Douglas Stewart's *The Fire on the Snow* in 1941.
4. See the *Argus* (Melbourne) 5th November 1928; the *Bulletin* (Sydney) 7th November 1928, p. 17.
5. For a discussion of this play, see Leslie Rees, *The Making of Australian Drama*, p. 189.
6. This is the cast as it appears in the 1942 publication (which, however omits mention of Reg Moyle as Harry.) The original programme, of which there is a copy in the State Library of Victoria, names Eric Donald as having played David Ritchie, and other names are spelled differently: Shappere, Claud Thomas, David Dorritty.
7. Detailed in Note 4 above.
8. The two major box office successes were *The Squatter's Daughter*, a melodrama by Bert Bailey and Edmund Duggan, and *On Our Selection*, Steele Rudd's bucolic comedy adapted for the stage by

the author in collaboration with Bert Bailey. It is interesting to note that plays such as these were taken as the touchstones at a time when the Pioneer Players, now generally regarded as the first sign of life for serious Australian drama, were barely two years disbanded. The reference here to "superior literary efforts" is exceptional; for. most of the reviewers of *The Touch of Silk*, the plays of Esson, Prichard, Palmer and their ilk might never have been performed. Similarly, the phenomenon of the extremely popular commercial productions of the nineteenth century is passed over in silence.

9. 30th October 1929. The *Daily Telegraph Pictorial* (Sydney), 28th October 1929, in a brief notice of the play, called it "a woman's play".

10. See the *Bulletin* review of *The Touch of Silk*, and also The *Sydney Morning Herald's* review of Goldoni's *Mine Hostess* at the Turret, 22nd July 1,929. *The Touch of Silk* was the first Australian play produced at the Turret Theatre, which had opened in March 1929. The production was designed and directed by Don Finley, who had worked for the Pioneers in Melbourne and was to achieve a degree of prominence as a theatre designer in Sydney and later in London.

11. In 1934, Betty Roland met Constantia Derjavin, director of the Alexandrinsky Theatre in Leningrad, who read *The Touch of Silk* and liked it well enough to offer her a contract and several hundred roubles advance royalties. The intended production on the Little Stage of that celebrated theatre failed to materialise largely because of the repercussions from the assassination of Sergei Kirov later that year. In 1943, two prominent New York entrepreneurs bought an option, and there was talk of Elizabeth Bergner as Jeanne. The difficulty of communication between continents in wartime led to the project being dropped. And again in 1955, Jack De Lion of the Q Theatre, London, contracted to produce the play; but he died suddenly and the theatre went out of production.

12. See Leslie Rees, *The Making of Australian Drama*, Chapters X to XII for an account of radio drama in Australia.

13. The first production preceded the establishment of the ABC's Productions Department, and no details of it survive. The play was produced three times in Melbourne (April 1938, July 1950, July 1957), four times in Perth (September 1938, June 1940, June 1944,

November 1953), twice in Sydney (December 1942, April 1947), three times in Brisbane (May 1949, May 1950, January 1957) and twice in Launceston (January 1949, June 1956).

14. The American version was made by an enterprising director who, having met Betty Roland during the War, produced the play in his local playhouse in Winchester, Virginia. The author did not see the adaptation until after the production, which was in the mid–'fifties, and was not at all pleased with it. At about the same time, she completed her own adaptation, bringing the play up to date. Some of the revisions to be found in A were made in this version, but as one would expect, there are even more substantial divergences, For instance, Jeanne hails from a farm on the Loire, and her memories are of a friendlier, more picturesque countryside rather than of metropolitan pleasures; and in general the characters, especially Mrs Davidson, are more genial. A manuscript of this version is held by the author; it has never been performed.

www.currency.com.au

Visit Currency Press' website now to:

- Order books
- Browse through our full list of titles including plays, screenplays, theory and reference/criticism, performance handbooks, educational texts and more
- Choose a play for your school or performance group by cast specs
- Seek performance rights
- Find out about performing arts news and sign up for our newsletter
- For students: read our study guides
- For teachers: access free curriculum information and teacher notes

We are also on Facebook and Instagram (@currencypress). Join the conversation!

The performing arts publisher